Step Forward
Language for Everyday Life

Multilevel Activity Book

SERIES DIRECTOR
Jayme Adelson-Goldstein

D1568656

Introductory Level

Chris Armen Mahdesian

OXFORD
UNIVERSITY PRESS

OXFORD
UNIVERSITY PRESS

198 Madison Avenue
New York, NY 10016 USA

Great Clarendon Street, Oxford OX2 6DP UK

Oxford University Press is a department of the University of Oxford.
It furthers the University's objective of excellence in research,
scholarship, and education by publishing worldwide in

Oxford New York

Auckland Cape Town Dar es Salaam Hong Kong Karachi
Kuala Lumpur Madrid Melbourne Mexico City Nairobi
New Delhi Shanghai Taipei Toronto

With offices in

Argentina Austria Brazil Chile Czech Republic France Greece
Guatemala Hungary Italy Japan Poland Portugal Singapore
South Korea Switzerland Thailand Turkey Ukraine Vietnam

Oxford and Oxford English are registered trademarks of
Oxford University Press

© Oxford University Press 2008

Database right Oxford University Press (maker)

Editorial Director: Sally Yagan
Senior Publishing Manager: Stephanie Karras
Head of Project and Development Editors: Karen Horton
Managing Editor: Sharon Sargent
Associate Project Editor: Meredith Stoll
Design Director: Robert Carangelo
Design Project Manager: Maj-Britt Hagsted
Project Manager: Allison Harm
Production Layout Artist: Julie Armstrong
Production Manager: Shanta Persaud
Production Controller: Zai Jawat Ali
Packager: Bill Smith Studio

Printed in Hong Kong

10 9 8 7 6 5 4 3 2 1

ISBN: 978 0 19 439848 0

Art Credits:

Argosy Publishing: 15, 16, 25, 43, 44, 59, 63, 64, 73, 74, 80, 81, 133, 134
Shawn Banner: 28, 69, 88, 98, 115, 128, 129 Niki Barolini: 19, 48 Kenneth
Batelman: 109, 119 John Batten: 13, 58, 93, 94 Kathy Baxendale: 53, 54,
114, Arlene Boehm: 29, 38 Richard Carbajal/illustrationonline.com: 55,
103, 104, 113, 123, 124 Bill Dickson/Contactjupiter.com: 23, 24, 33, 34,
39, 45, 75, 85, 95, 99, 105, 108, 118, 125, 135, Geo Parkin: 18, 49, 68, 78
Ron Zalme: 35, 65, 79, 89

Photo Credits:
Dennis Kitchen Studio: 1.

With special thanks to Kathryn O'Shields
for her many valuable contributions,
Sharon Sargent for entrusting me with
MLABi, Genevieve Kocienda for polishing
up the details, Meredith Stoll for pulling it
all together, and last but not least, Jayme
Adelson-Goldstein and Jane Spigarelli without
whom, none of this would be possible.
This book is dedicated to teachers and their
work as individuals for making a difference
and changing the lives of those they serve for
the better, each and every day.

Chris

Kudos to the Intro Multilevel Activity Book
team members for creating another celestial
body in the Step Forward universe: Chris
Mahesdian-authorial font of creative thought;
Kathryn O'Shields-development editor par
excellence; Meredith Stoll and Genevieve
Kocienda-production editors with panache;
and Sharon Sargent-star maker.
Special thanks to Chris-who cares so deeply
about everything he does.

Jayme

Acknowledgments

Curriculum Consultant
Kathy Santopietro Weddel
Northern Colorado Literacy Program, Littleton, CO

The Publisher and Series Director would like to acknowledge the following individuals for their invaluable input during the development of this series:

Robert Anzelde Triton College, River Grove, IL

Patricia Bell Lake Technical Center, Eustis, FL

Curtis Bonney North Seattle Community College, Seattle, WA

Ana Patricia Castro Harvest English Institute, Newark, NJ

Edwidge Bryant University of North Florida, Jacksonville, FL

Julie Caspersen Old Marshall Adult Education Center, Sacramento, CA

Bart Chaney Dallas Independent School District, Dallas, TX

Kathleen Fallon Clackamas Community College, Oregon City, OR

Cheryl L. Fuentes ESOL Consultant, Alexandria, VA

Carol Garcia College of DuPage, Glen Ellyn, IL

Ann Jackson Mid Florida Tech, Orlando, FL

Gaye Kendall Harris County Department of Education, Houston, TX

Jennifer Martin Baldwin Park Adult and Community Education, Baldwin Park, CA

Suzi Monti Community College of Baltimore County, Baltimore, MD

Rob Patton Communities in Schools—Central Texas, Austin, TX

Linda A. Pelc New York City Department of Education, New York, NY

Marvina Pérez Hooper Lake Technical Center, Eustis, FL

David L. Red Fairfax County Public Schools, Falls Church, VA

Barbara Sample Spring Institute for Intercultural Learning, Denver, CO

Denise Selleck City College of San Francisco—Alemany, San Francisco, CA

Esther Shupe Brookdale Community College, Long Branch, NJ

Margaret B. Silver English Language and Literacy Center, Clayton, MO

Melissa Singler Cape Fear Community College, Wilmington, NC

Betty Stone Somerville Center for Adult Learning Experiences, Somerville, MA

Maliheh Vafai Overfelt Adult Center, San Jose, CA

Cynthia Wiseman Borough of Manhattan Community College, New York, NY

We would also like to thank the following students in the Fall 2006 Beginning Literacy Class at ABC Adult School in Cerritos, CA.

Emelia Alvarez	Jung Soon Jung	Maria Luisa Lopez
Virej Benyamin	Jin Shik Kim	Kai Pang Ng
Liang-Ming Chen	Kil Su Kim	Ga Young Oh
Li Yu Chen	Soon Hi Kim	Oknyu Park
Yang Ja Choi	Soon Yi Kim	Sun Soon Park
Soon Hee Chong	In Taek Lee	Sung Ja Park
Chi-Yu Chou Chiu	Jung So Lee	Young Sun Park
Lotai Chung	Myung Yong Lee	Norma Talavera Riviera
Somath Oeurn Dell	Ok Ja Lee	Zaihong Shen
Adulfo Garcia	Tae Soo Lee	Angelica Torres
Kyung Soon Han	Wan Chen Lee	Min Chen Wang
Shu-yeh Hsu	Phourngmalay Long	Tzu Tseng Wang
Hee Sik Im	Vanny Long	Keum Soon Woo
Jin Taek Jung	David Lopez	Young Ja Yoo

Contents

Introduction to the *Step Forward Multilevel Activity Book Introductory Level*

Welcome to the *Step Forward Multilevel Activity Book Introductory Level*. In these pages you'll find a wealth of highly interactive activities that require little preparation. All of the activities can be used in numerous ways with a variety of learners. The 110 activities in this book are effective in beginning classes as well as in multilevel classes with learners ranging from newcomers to low-intermediate levels.

This book is divided into 12 units that directly correspond to *Step Forward Student Book Introductory Level*. Each activity supports and expands upon the student book's lesson objectives, for a complete approach to English language learning.

1 What is the Multilevel Activity Book?

The *Multilevel Activity Book Introductory Level* (like the entire *Step Forward* series) is based on research that says adults taught in a learner-centered classroom retain more material for longer periods of time (McCombs and Whistler, 1997; Benson and Voller, 1997). Through its guided and communicative practice opportunities, the *Multilevel Activity Book Introductory Level* provides hours of meaningful and fun classroom activities.

2 How do I use these reproducible activities?

The Teaching Notes on pages 3–11 give detailed directions on how to conduct each activity. They also provide multilevel suggestions, guiding you through

1. setting up the activity,
2. modeling/demonstrating the activity, and
3. checking your learners' comprehension of each activity's goal and directions.

Once learners understand how to proceed, they are able to work together to complete the activities. Putting learning into the learners' hands is an important step toward ensuring that they will achieve the lesson objective. Moving away from the front-and-center role frees you to circulate, monitor, facilitate, and gain insight into how well the lesson information was captured. You discover what learners can and can't do well, and adjust your future lesson plans accordingly.

3 What makes these activities multilevel?

One of the key techniques in multilevel instruction is to use materials that can work

The Peer Dictation activity allows learners to work at their own level and pace to perform the same task. Higher-level pairs dictate additional words from the unit for further listening and speaking practice, while lower-level pairs spell out the words to each other to reinforce their clarification and spelling skills.

across levels. There are eight activity types in this book. Each one allows you to tailor practice to the learner's abilities, but still have the entire class working on the same basic activity. (See the photo on page one for an example.) Having only eight activity types means that students quickly understand how to do the activities, requiring less teacher intervention and more learner-directed practice. Each activity includes a Keep Going suggestion in the Teaching Notes for a follow-up activity, such as graphing results, discussing answers and writing more about the picture in the activity. The eight activity types are described below.

ACTIVITY	GROUPING STRATEGY	DESCRIPTION	CORRELATION TO *Step Forward Student Book Introductory Level*
Round Table Label	Small Groups	Learners take turns labeling unit vocabulary in a scene.	**Lesson 1: Vocabulary**
Find and Circle	Pairs	Learners work together to circle items in a scene using a word bank. Then the pairs use the words to complete sentences about the scene.	**Lesson 2: Life stories**
Sentence Maker	Small Groups	Learners use word cards to make five different sentences or questions in ten minutes.	**Lesson 3: Grammar**
Role-Play	Small Groups	Learners develop fluency by practicing and expanding upon conversation gambits.	**Lesson 4: Everyday conversation**
Mixer	Whole Class	Learners get acquainted as they ask and answer questions.	**Lesson 5: Real-life reading**
Picture Cards	Pairs	Partners use flash cards to study the unit's target vocabulary.	**Review and expand**
Look and Say	Whole Class	Learners work together to describe a scene, and the teacher writes their ideas on the board. Learners then practice writing by copying the description.	**Review and expand**
Peer Dictation	Pairs	Partners take turns dictating words or sentences that reinforce grammar structures while developing their clarification strategies.	**Review and expand**

By having pairs or small groups practice the language required to meet a lesson objective, teachers facilitate learners' use and internalization of the target language. This also provides important opportunities for learners to engage in real-life interaction strategies such as negotiating meaning, checking information, disagreeing, and reaching consensus.

While a pair of running shoes is not required equipment, most multilevel instructors find themselves on the move in the classroom.

These highly structured activities support the energetic, communicative, and lively approach to learning that is the hallmark of effective multilevel instruction. The Step Forward Team hopes that you and your learners enjoy these activities.

Please write to us with your comments and questions: **Stepforwardteam.us@oup.com.**

Jayme Adelson-Goldstein

Jayme Adelson-Goldstein, Series Director

Multilevel Activity Teaching Notes

Teaching Notes for the Round Table Label

Focus: Students use lesson vocabulary to label items in a picture.
Grouping Strategy: Groups of 4 students
Activity Time: 20–25 minutes
Student Book Connection: Lesson 1

Ready,

1. Select the Round Table Label activity that corresponds to the unit you are teaching in *Step Forward Student Book Introductory Level*.

2. Duplicate one activity page for each group.

3. On the board, post three pictures or draw three objects related to the lesson topic. Draw a line next to each picture. (Students will write the name of the object on the blank line.)

Set . . .

1. Share the goal of the activity: *You're going to work together to label items in a picture.*

2. Form groups of four students.

3. Model the activity. Have one group come forward and take turns passing the chalk and labeling the pictures on the board. Point out that students can label any picture or object they choose.

4. Once all the pictures are labeled, have the class check the students' spelling in *The Oxford Picture Dictionary* or another dictionary.

5. Distribute one activity page to each group and review the directions.

6. To reinforce the circulation of the activity page within the group, have group members pass their activity page from student to student, writing their names at the top of the page.

7. Check students' comprehension by asking *yes/no* questions. Act out the questions as you ask them. *Does one person write all the words on the paper?* [no] *Do you pass the paper to the person next to you?* [yes]

Go!

1. Set a time limit (ten minutes). Tell students not to worry about spelling for now. They will check their spelling later.

2. Each student labels one vocabulary item and then passes the sheet to another group member. Students continue taking turns until they've labeled all the items they know.

3. Monitor progress and encourage students to ask their group members for help if they are unsure of a word or its spelling.

4. Call "time" and have students check the spelling of each word in *The Oxford Picture Dictionary* or another dictionary.

5. Elicit the answers and write them on the board. Or make a transparency of the activity page and have volunteers take turns labeling the picture.

Keep Going!

Elicit anything else students can say about the picture. Write their words and sentences on the board and read them together as a class.

Multilevel Suggestions

For Mixed-Level Groups:
Tell pre-level students that they can say rather than write the words. Instruct on-level and higher-level students to write their pre-level group members' ideas on the activity page.

For Same-Level Groups:
Pre-Level: Give each group of students a list of the words matching the blanks in the picture. Have them complete the activity as outlined above, using the word list for help as needed.

On-Level: Have students complete the activity as outlined above.

Higher-Level: Place the picture in the middle of the group and have students pass around a sheet of notebook paper. Ask them to take turns writing sentences about the picture.

Teaching Notes for Find and Circle

Focus: Using a word bank, students identify and circle items in a scene. They then use the words to complete sentences about the picture.
Grouping Strategy: Pairs
Activity Time: 15–20 minutes
Student Book Connection: Lesson 2

Ready,

1. Select the Find and Circle activity that corresponds to the unit you are teaching in *Step Forward Student Book Introductory Level*.

2. Duplicate one activity page for each pair.

3. On the board, draw a scene containing three objects related to the lesson topic. Draw a box above the scene with the names of the objects in it. (Students will cross out each word as they circle the corresponding object in the picture.)

Set . . .

1. Share the goal of the activity: *First, you're going to work with a partner to read the words in the box and circle what you find in the picture. Then you're going to complete some sentences about the picture.*

2. Model the activity. Point to and read aloud the first word in the box above the scene drawn on the board. Circle that item in the picture. Cross out the word in the box.

3. Have volunteers come to the board and repeat the process for the remaining two words.

4. Check comprehension by asking *yes/no* questions. Act out the questions as you ask them. *Does one student find and circle all of the words?* [no] *Can you help your partner find and circle the objects in the picture?* [yes]

5. Distribute the activity page and review the instructions for the second part of the activity. Write a skeleton sentence on the board that is related to the scene you drew. Elicit and write the answer. Read the completed sentence aloud.

6. Check comprehension by asking *yes/no* questions. Act out the questions as you ask them. *Does one student complete all the sentences?* [no] *Can you help your partner complete the sentences below the picture?* [yes]

Go!

1. Review the directions.

2. Set a time limit (fifteen minutes) for partners to find and circle the items from the word box and complete the sentences about the picture.

3. Call "time" and check students' accuracy.

4. Have volunteers read the completed sentences aloud. Write them on the board.

Keep Going!

Have students form groups and write additional sentences about the picture together. Ask volunteers to write their sentences on the board.

Multilevel Suggestions

For Mixed-Level Pairs:
Pair higher-level or on-level students with pre-level students. Have higher-level students read the words in the box. Have pre-level students circle the objects in the picture.

For Same-Level Pairs:
Pre-Level: Seat these students together and give each student a copy of the activity page. Read the words in the box aloud and have the students circle the objects in the picture.

On-Level: Have students complete the activity as outlined above.

Higher-Level: Have these students write additional sentences and/or questions about the picture.

Teaching Notes for the Sentence Maker

Focus: Students work in groups to make five different sentences or questions using word cards.
Grouping Strategy: Groups of 3–4 students
Activity Time: 15–20 minutes
Student Book Connection: Lesson 3

Ready,

1. Select the Sentence Maker activity that corresponds to the unit you are teaching in *Step Forward Student Book Introductory Level*.

2. Duplicate one activity page for each group. Have scissors on hand for each group.

3. Cut apart one set of word cards for modeling the activity.

4. Draw these six sample "cards" on the board:

SHE	NOT	IS
STUDENT	A	.

Set . . .

1. Share the goal of the activity: *You're going to work together to make five sentences or questions using word cards.*

2. Point out the punctuation card. Elicit a sentence using the sample cards on the board. Write the sentence on the board.

3. Have several students at the front of the room model the activity as you explain it. Ask the class to watch and listen.

• *The group works with the cards to make a sentence.*

• *They dictate the sentence to the group's Recorder.*

• *The Recorder writes the sentence and reads it to the group. Then the group repeats the process, making more sentences.*

4. Check comprehension by asking *yes/no* questions. Act out the questions as you ask them. *Do you write on the cards?* [no] *Do you make more than one sentence?* [yes]

5. Form groups of three or four students and have each group choose a Recorder.

Go!

1. Distribute one set of cards and a pair of scissors to each group and review the directions.

2. Have each group cut apart the word cards.

3. Set a time limit (ten minutes) and have groups begin the activity.

4. Monitor and facilitate the group work.

5. Call "time." Ask Recorders to tell how many sentences the group wrote.

Keep Going!

Have each group write two or three of their sentences on the board. Ask the class to give feedback on the accuracy of the sentences.

Multilevel Suggestions

For Mixed-Level Groups:
Create groups that have at least one higher-level student who can serve as the Recorder. Ask on-level and higher-level students to help pre-level students read the sentences once they are written.

For Same-Level Groups:
Pre-Level: Give the group a list of sentences that can be made from the cards. Have students assemble matching sentences with the cards, checking off each sentence on the list as they make it.

On-Level: Have students complete the activity as outlined above.

Higher-Level: Have students look at the list of sentences they created and make new sentences by changing one word. Or have them write a corresponding question for each sentence.

Teaching Notes for the Role-Play

Focus: Student groups read a script, choose roles, write the ending, and act out a role-play.
Grouping Strategy: Groups of 3–4 students
Activity Time: 45–60 minutes
Student Book Connection: Lesson 4

Ready,

1. Select the Role-Play activity that corresponds to the unit you are teaching in *Step Forward Student Book Introductory Level.*

2. Duplicate one activity page for each student.

3. Check the "Props" list to determine what items you need to bring to class. Each group will need its own set of props.

4. Check the script to determine what, if any, new vocabulary students will need in order to do the role-play.

Set . . .

1. Share the goal of the activity: *You're going to work in groups and act out different parts in a role-play.*

2. Have students form groups according to the number of characters.

3. Distribute one activity page per person and one set of props per group. Review the directions: *First, read the script. Next, decide who will play each character. Then write an ending. You must add lines for each character.*

4. Present new vocabulary or review vocabulary as needed.

5. Model the role-play. Play one of the characters yourself to demonstrate the use of gestures and expression. Have student volunteers read the other parts. Elicit ways to complete the role-play.

6. Check comprehension by asking *yes/no* questions. Act out the questions as you ask them. *Do you say all the lines?* [no] *Do you act out your lines?* [yes] *Do you write more lines?* [yes]

Go!

1. Set a time limit (fifteen minutes) for the group to read the script, choose their characters, and finish the role-play.

2. Set a time limit (ten minutes) and have the students act out the role-play in their groups.

3. Monitor students' progress by walking around and helping with pronunciation problems. Encourage pantomime and improvisation.

Keep Going!

Have each group perform their role-play for the class. After each performance, ask students who are watching *yes/no* questions about what they saw and heard.

Multilevel Suggestions

For Mixed-Level Groups:
Adapt the role-play to include a non-speaking or limited speaking role for pre-level students who are not ready to participate verbally. For example, add a character who only answers *yes* or *no* to questions asked by another character.

For Same-Level Groups:
Pre-Level: On the board, write a simplified conversation based on the role-play situation. Help students read and copy the conversation in their notebooks. Then have pairs practice the conversation until they can perform it without the script.

On-Level: Have students complete the activity as outlined above.

Higher-Level: Have students write a new role-play using related vocabulary or a similar situation.

Teaching Notes for the Mixer

Focus: Students get to know each other by asking and answering questions.
Grouping Strategy: Whole class
Activity Time: 25–30 minutes
Student Book Connection: Lesson 5

Ready,

1. Select the Mixer activity that corresponds to the unit you are teaching in *Step Forward Student Book Introductory Level*.

2. Duplicate one activity page for each student.

3. Copy the column heads and the first three rows of the chart on the board.

Set . . .

1. Share the goal of the activity: *You're going to talk to your classmates to complete the Mixer.*

2. Model the activity. Ask a student the question and complete the first row of the chart on the board with the required information. When you need to write a student's name in the chart, ask the student to spell the name slowly as you write it.

3. Have a volunteer complete the second row of the chart on the board by asking you the question. Have a different volunteer complete the third row by asking another student.

4. Distribute an activity page to each student and review the directions.

5. Check students' comprehension by asking *yes/no* questions. Act out the questions as you ask them. *Do you answer the questions yourself?* [no] *Do you write your name in the chart?* [no]

Go!

1. Set a time limit (10 minutes).

2. Have students circulate to complete the activity page. Tell them to sit down when their chart is complete.

3. Enter the mixer yourself. Students will enjoy your participation, and you can check their accuracy.

4. Give students a two-minute warning before time is up.

5. Call "time."

Keep Going!

Talk about the results of the mixer with the class.

Multilevel Suggestions

Before the activity:
Pre-Level: Help students read the question(s) and write their own answers in their notebooks.
On-Level: Have students read the question(s) and write their own answers in their notebooks.
Higher-Level: Pair students and have them write three to five new questions on the Mixer topic to add to their activity page.

During the activity:
On-level and higher-level students can stay "in the mix" by helping pre-level students once their own activity page is complete.

Teaching Notes for the Picture Cards

Focus: Students review key vocabulary using picture cards for flash cards.
Grouping Strategy: Pairs
Activity Time: Various
Student Book Connection: Review and Expand

Ready,

1. Select the Picture Cards that correspond to the unit you are teaching in *Step Forward Student Book Introductory Level.*

2. Duplicate one page of Picture Cards for each pair. Have scissors on hand for each pair.

3. Cut apart one of the Picture Card pages to use in the demonstration.

Set . . .

1. Share the goal of the activity: *You will use flashcards to practice vocabulary.*

2. Pair students and give each pair a copy of the activity page. Hold up one Picture Card and elicit the word. Direct students to find the word in the word list. Write the word on the back of the card. Hold up another card and elicit where to write the word.

3. Have pairs cut apart the picture cards and write the corresponding word from the word list on the reverse side of each card.

4. Review vocabulary as needed.

5. Model the activity for the class. Ask a volunteer to hold up a picture card. Say the corresponding word or phrase. Tell the volunteer to look at the back of the card to check whether you are correct. Change roles.

Go!

1. Assign A/B roles.

2. Partner A holds up a picture card. Partner B says the corresponding vocabulary word or phrase. Partner A looks at the reverse side of the card to verify accuracy. Then the students change roles.

3. Allow students to keep their cards for future study.

Keep Going!

Have pairs form groups of four and take turns using the flash cards to see who can name the most words in the shortest time.

Multilevel Suggestions

For Mixed-Level Pairs:
Have the on-level or higher-level student say all of the words first. Then ask the pre-level student to point to the correct picture as their partner says the words.

For Same-Level Pairs:
Pre-Level: Work with these students separately to review all the pictures. Have students point to or hold up the pictures as first you, then volunteers, say the word or describe the picture.

On-Level: Have students complete the activities as outlined above.

Higher-Level: Ask these students to use each of the words in a sentence.

Teaching Notes for Look and Say

Focus: Students work as a class to describe a scene. The teacher writes the description on the board for the class to copy.
Grouping Strategy: Whole class
Activity Time: 25–35 minutes
Student Book Connection: Review and Expand

Ready,

1. Select the Look and Say activity that corresponds to the unit you are teaching in *Step Forward Student Book Introductory Level*.

2. Duplicate one activity page for each student.

Set . . .

1. Share the goal of the activity: *We are going to write what we see in this picture.*

2. Distribute the activity sheet.

3. Ask students to say as much as they can about the picture. Elicit several ideas to get them started.

4. Check comprehension by asking questions. Act out the questions as you ask them. *Do you write?* [no] *Do you say words?* [yes] *Do you say sentences?* [yes]

Go!

1. Set a time limit (10 minutes) for students to look at and talk about the picture with the class.

2. Call "time."

3. Elicit their ideas. When a student provides only a word or a phrase, call on another volunteer to complete the sentence. Help students along by asking *yes/no* and short answer questions with familiar vocabulary (e.g., *Is this a man or a woman? Where is she?*). Write their ideas as a story on the board. Direct students not to copy the story until it is finished.

4. When the story is finished, read it together as a class. Ask if students would like to make any additions or changes. Have them copy the story into their notebooks.

Keep Going!

Have students take turns reading the story aloud with a partner.

Multilevel Suggestions

For Mixed-Level Groups:
Elicit ideas from on-level and higher-level students first, encouraging them to use any words or phrases they can to describe the picture. Then call on pre-level students to point to the relevant part of the picture. Have higher-level students develop their classmates' ideas into sentences for you to write on the board.

For Same-Level Groups:
Pre-Level: Have students suggest words or phrases rather than sentences to describe the picture.

On-Level: Have students complete the activity as outlined above.

Higher-Level: Have students take turns writing their classmates' sentences on the board.

Teaching Notes for Peer Dictation

Focus: Students dictate words or sentences to each other.
Grouping Strategy: Pairs
Activity Time: 15–25 minutes
Student Book Connection: Review and Expand

Ready,

1. Select the Peer Dictation activity that corresponds to the unit you are teaching in *Step Forward Student Book Introductory Level*.

2. Duplicate one activity page for each student.

3. On the left side of the board, write a word that relates to the topic. Label this side of the board *Partner A*. Label the right side of the board *Partner B*.

4. Familiarize students with the dictation process by asking a volunteer to read the word on the left side of the board to you. As you write the word on the right side of the board, model a clarification strategy, e.g., *Can you spell that, please?* or *Can you repeat that, please?*

Set . . .

1. Share the goal of the activity: *You're going to practice reading, listening to, and writing words.*

2. Pair students. Have one volunteer pair model the activity for the class. Ask the pair to come to the front of the class and sit across from each other. Give each partner one of the activity pages. Assign A/B roles to the volunteer partners. Tell the partners what to do as the class watches and listens.

- *Fold your papers.*
- *Partner A, look at the top. Partner B, look at the bottom.*
- *Partner A, read the first word (or sentence) on the page to your partner. Repeat it.*
- *Partner B, write the word.*

3. When A finishes, have B dictate the first word or sentence on the bottom half of the sheet to A.

4. Check comprehension by asking *or* questions. Act out the questions as you ask them. *Do you fold or cut the paper?* [fold] *Does Partner A read the A words/sentences or the B words/sentences?* [the A words/sentences]

Go!

1. Distribute one activity page per person and review the directions.

2. Assign *A/B* roles to each pair and have them fold their activity pages.

3. Set a time limit (five minutes) for A to dictate to B.

4. Call "time" and set a time limit (five minutes) for B to dictate to A.

5. Call "time" and have pairs unfold their papers and check their work

Keep Going!

Have pairs create three new sentences on the same topic as the Peer Dictation. Call on volunteers to read one of the sentences to the class.

Multilevel Suggestions

For Mixed-Level Pairs:
Pair on-level or higher-level students with pre-level students. Allow pre-level students to either write or to dictate, depending on what they would rather do.

For Same-Level Pairs:
Pre-Level: Have students spell the words instead of reading them.

On-Level: Have students complete the activity as outlined above.

Higher-Level: For single-word dictations, have each partner dictate additional words from the unit. For sentence dictations, have one partner dictate the sentence from the activity sheet while the other partner writes the complete sentence in a notebook.

Pre-Unit The First Step

Learn English!

1. Work with 3 classmates.

2. Label what you see in the picture.

3. Check your spelling in a dictionary.

KEEP GOING!

Talk about the picture. Say what you see.

Excuse Me?

1. Work with 2 classmates. Say all the lines in the script.

2. Choose your character.

3. Finish the conversation. Write more lines.

4. Practice the lines.

5. Act out the role-play with your group.

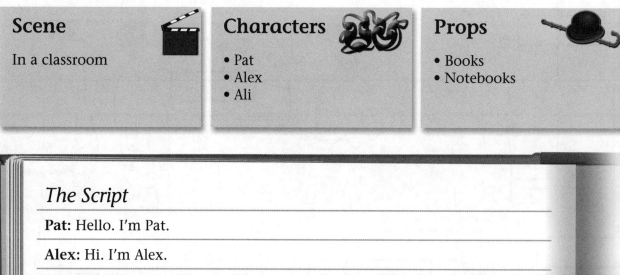

Scene

In a classroom

Characters

- Pat
- Alex
- Ali

Props

- Books
- Notebooks

The Script

Pat: Hello. I'm Pat.

Alex: Hi. I'm Alex.

Pat: Excuse me?

Alex: Alex. A-L-E-X.

Ali: Hello. I'm Ali.

Alex: Excuse me?

KEEP GOING!

Act out the role-play for your class.

Picture Cards

1. Cut apart the picture cards. Use the word list to write the words on the back.

2. Work with a partner.

   Partner A: Show the picture card to your partner.

   Partner B: Say the word.

3. Change roles.

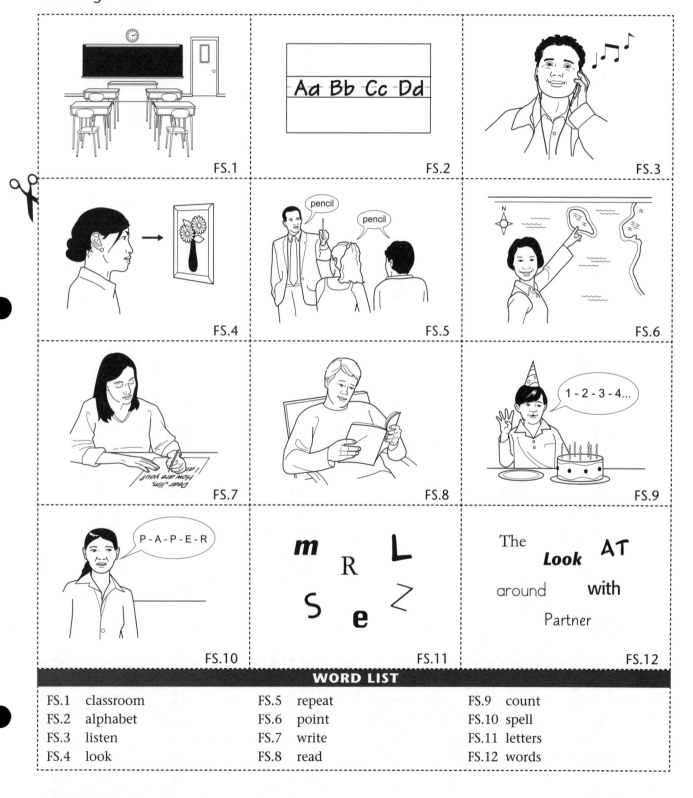

WORD LIST		
FS.1 classroom	FS.5 repeat	FS.9 count
FS.2 alphabet	FS.6 point	FS.10 spell
FS.3 listen	FS.7 write	FS.11 letters
FS.4 look	FS.8 read	FS.12 words

Picture Cards

1. Cut apart the picture cards. Use the word list to write the words on the back.

2. Work with a partner.

    Partner A: Show the picture card to your partner.

    Partner B: Say the word.

3. Change roles.

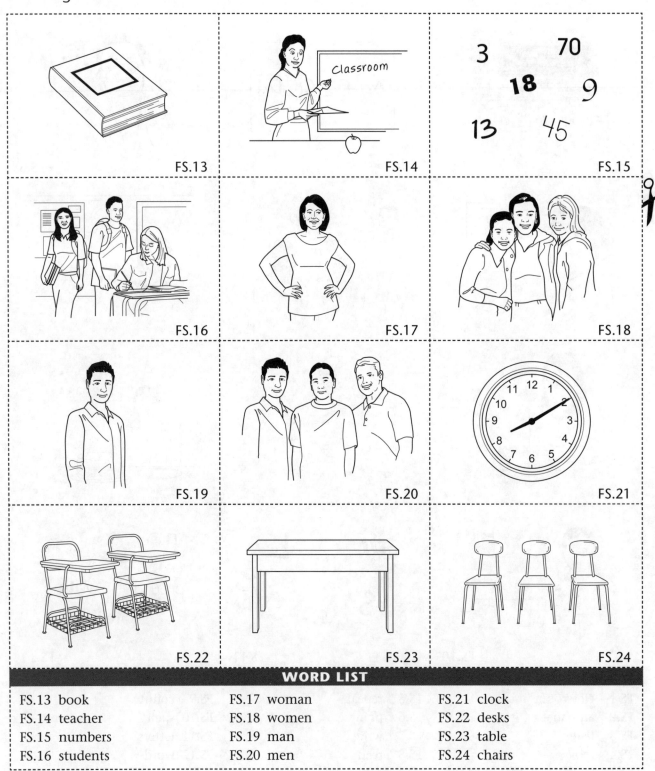

FS.13	FS.14	FS.15
FS.16	FS.17	FS.18
FS.19	FS.20	FS.21
FS.22	FS.23	FS.24

WORD LIST

FS.13 book	FS.17 woman	FS.21 clock
FS.14 teacher	FS.18 women	FS.22 desks
FS.15 numbers	FS.19 man	FS.23 table
FS.16 students	FS.20 men	FS.24 chairs

Unit 1 Nice to Meet You

At Work

1. Work with 3 classmates.

2. Label what you see in the picture.

3. Check your spelling in a dictionary.

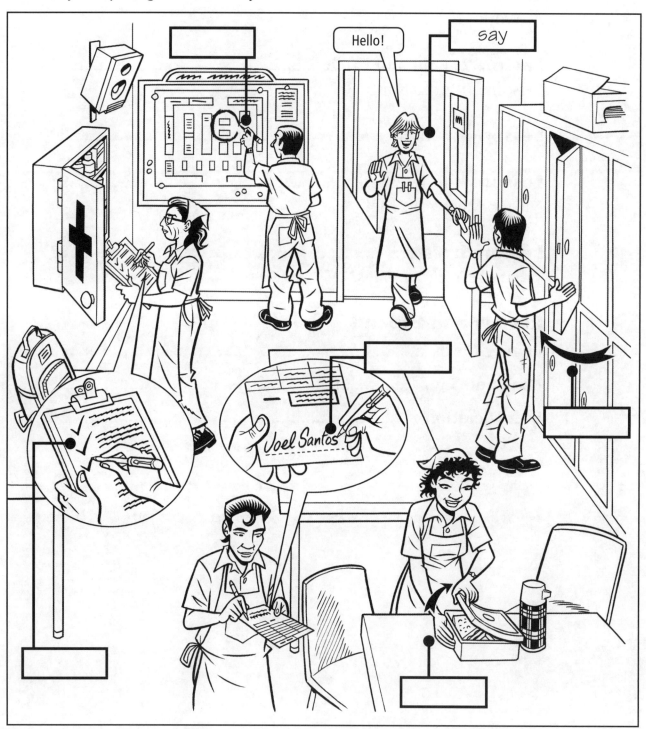

KEEP GOING!

Talk about the picture. Say what you see.

Personal Information

1. Work with a partner.

2. Read the words in the box.

3. Look at the picture. Circle what you see.

first name	middle name	last name	signature	~~check~~

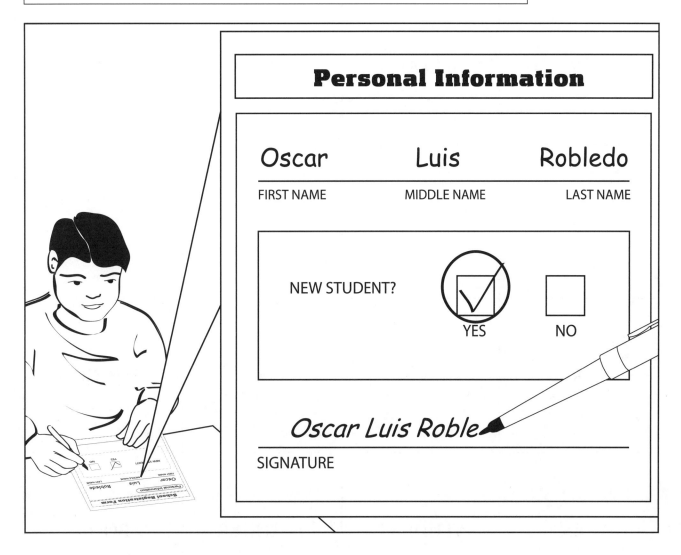

4. Look at the picture. Complete the sentences. Use *first name, last name,* or *middle name.*

The _____ is Luis.

The _____ is Robledo.

The _____ is Oscar.

KEEP GOING!

Work in a group. Write more about the picture.
Oscar is a student.

Sentence Maker

1. Work with a group of 3 or 4 students. Cut apart the cards.

2. Choose a Recorder.

3. Use the word cards to make 5 different sentences in 10 minutes. The Recorder writes the group's sentences.

I	YOU	HE	SHE
IT	WE	THEY	AM
ARE	IS	A	PENCIL
PEN	STUDENT	TEACHER	BOOK
STUDENTS	TEACHERS	BOOKS	.

Nice to Meet You, Too!

1. Work with 2 classmates. Say all the lines in the script.

3. Choose your character.

4. Finish the conversation. Write more lines.

5. Practice the lines.

6. Act out the role-play with your group.

Scene	**Characters**	**Props**
In a classroom	• Jin • Mel • Sam	• Books • Notebooks

The Script

Jin: Hello. I am Jin. What is your name?

Mel: My name is Mel.

Jin: Excuse me?

Mel: My name is Mel. M – E – L.

Jin: Nice to meet you, Mel.

Mel: Nice to meet you, too!

Jin: Sam is a student, too.

Sam: Hi. I am Sam.

Mel: Hello, Sam. You are my classmate.

Sam: Yes, I am.

Mel: What is your last name?

KEEP GOING!

Act out the role-play for your class.

What Are Your Supplies?

1. Walk around the room.

2. Ask your classmates: *Do you bring* _____ *to school?*

3. Write *yes* or *no* in the boxes for your classmates.

	Classmate 1	Classmate 2	Classmate 3	Classmate 4
Do you bring a pen to school?				
Do you bring a pencil to school?				
Do you bring an eraser to school?				
Do you bring a binder to school?				
Do you bring a notebook to school?				
Do you bring paper to school?				

KEEP GOING!

Talk about this mixer with your class.

Picture Cards

1. Cut apart the picture cards. Use the word list to write the words on the back.
2. Work with a partner.
   Partner A: Show the picture card to your partner.
   Partner B: Say the word.
3. Change roles.

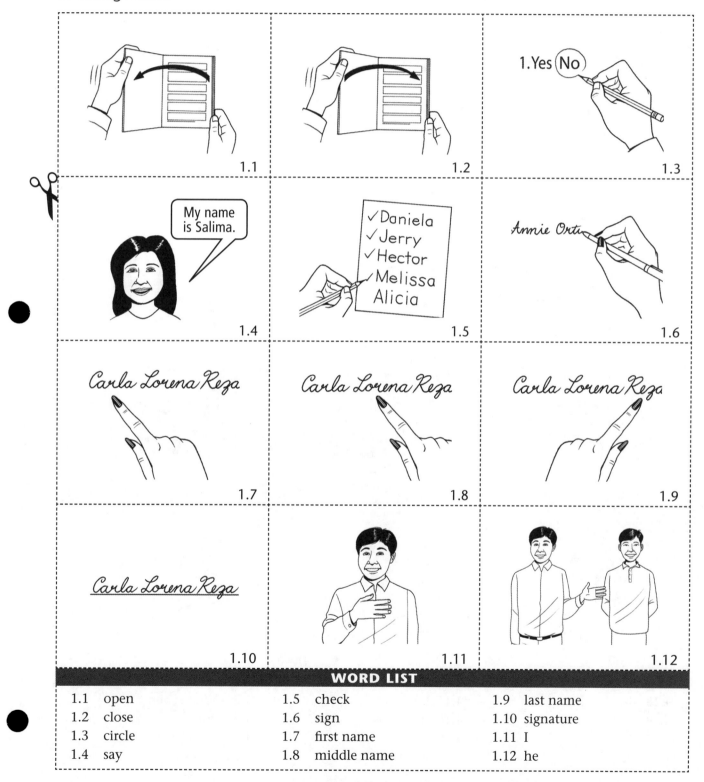

1.1	open	1.5	check	1.9	last name
1.2	close	1.6	sign	1.10	signature
1.3	circle	1.7	first name	1.11	I
1.4	say	1.8	middle name	1.12	he

Picture Cards

1. Cut apart the picture cards. Use the word list to write the words on the back.

2. Work with a partner.

   Partner A: Show the picture card to your partner.

   Partner B: Say the word.

3. Change roles.

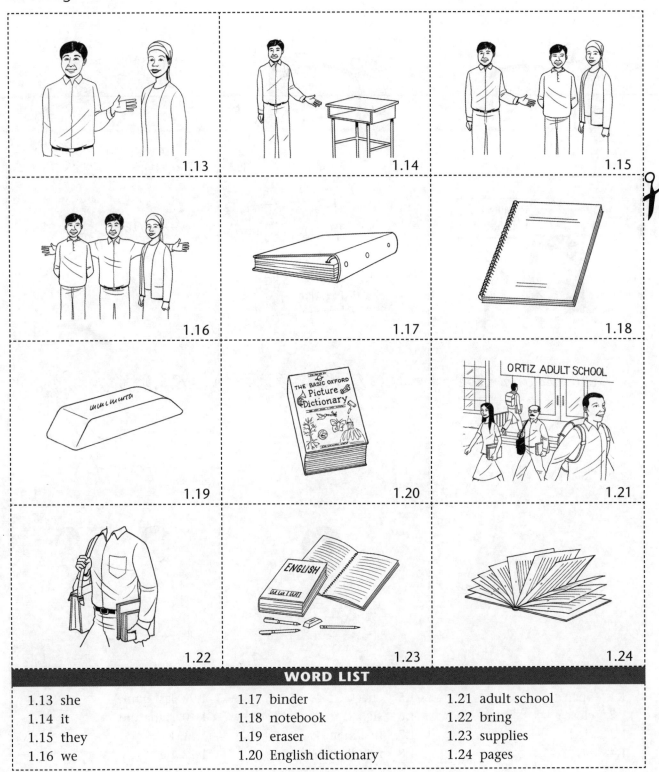

WORD LIST		
1.13 she	1.17 binder	1.21 adult school
1.14 it	1.18 notebook	1.22 bring
1.15 they	1.19 eraser	1.23 supplies
1.16 we	1.20 English dictionary	1.24 pages

In the Classroom

1. Work with your classmates.

2. Look at the picture.

3. Say what you see.

4. Watch your teacher write the story on the board or overhead.

5. Copy the story.

_____

_____

_____

_____

_____

_____

_____

_____

At School

Partner A
• **Read a word to Partner B.** • **Repeat the sentence.** • **Watch Partner B write the word.**
1. teacher 2. tables 3. classmates 4. pens
• **Listen to Partner B say a word.** • **Listen again.** • **Write the word.**
1.
2.
3.
4.

– FOLD HERE – – – – – – – – – – – – – – – – – – –

Partner B
• **Listen to Partner A say a word.** • **Listen again.** • **Write the word.**
1.
2.
3.
4.
• **Read a word to Partner A.** • **Repeat the word.** • **Watch Partner A write the word.**
1. binders 2. notebook 3. eraser 4. paper

Unit 2 How Are You Feeling?

Feelings

1. Work with 3 classmates.

2. Label what you see in the picture.

3. Check your spelling in a dictionary.

KEEP GOING!

Talk about the picture. Say what you see.

Where Is Mai From?

1. Work with a partner.

2. Read the words in the box.

3. Look at the picture. Circle what you see.

city	state	birthplace	country	first name	~~last name~~

4. Look at the picture. Complete the sentences. Use *China, Texas,* or *Wong.*

The last name is _____.

Mai is from _____.

Now Mai is in Dallas, _____.

KEEP GOING!

Work in a group. Write more about the picture.
Mai is a student.

Sentence Maker

1. Work with a group of 3 or 4 students. Cut apart the cards.

2. Choose a Recorder.

3. Use the word cards to make 5 different sentences in 10 minutes.
The Recorder writes the group's sentences.

I'M	YOU'RE	HE'S	SHE'S
IT'S	WE'RE	THEY'RE	NOT
FROM	A	HAPPY	HUNGRY
TIRED	CITY	STATE	COUNTRY
TEXAS	CHINA	MEXICO	.

I'm Not Hungry

1. Work with 2 classmates. Say all the lines in the script.

2. Choose your character.

3. Finish the conversation. Write more lines.

4. Practice the lines.

5. Act out the role-play with your group.

Scene	**Characters**	**Props**
At school	• Terry • Drew • Chris	Books or notebooks

The Script

Terry: How are you feeling?

Drew: I'm thirsty. How are you feeling?

Terry: We're hungry.

Chris: I'm not hungry.

Terry: Oh, I'm sorry. How are you feeling?

KEEP GOING!

Act out the role-play for your class.

Unit 2 Role-Play   **31**

What Is Your Zip Code?

1. Walk around the room.

2. Ask your classmates: *What is your zip code?*

3. Write the classmates' names. Write the zip codes.

	Name	Zip Code
Classmate 1		
Classmate 2		
Classmate 3		
Classmate 4		
Classmate 5		
Classmate 6		
Classmate 7		
Classmate 8		
Classmate 9		
Classmate 10		

KEEP GOING!

Talk about this mixer with your class.

Picture Cards

1. Cut apart the picture cards. Use the word list to write the words on the back.

2. Work with a partner.

    Partner A: Show the picture card to your partner.

    Partner B: Say the word.

3. Change roles.

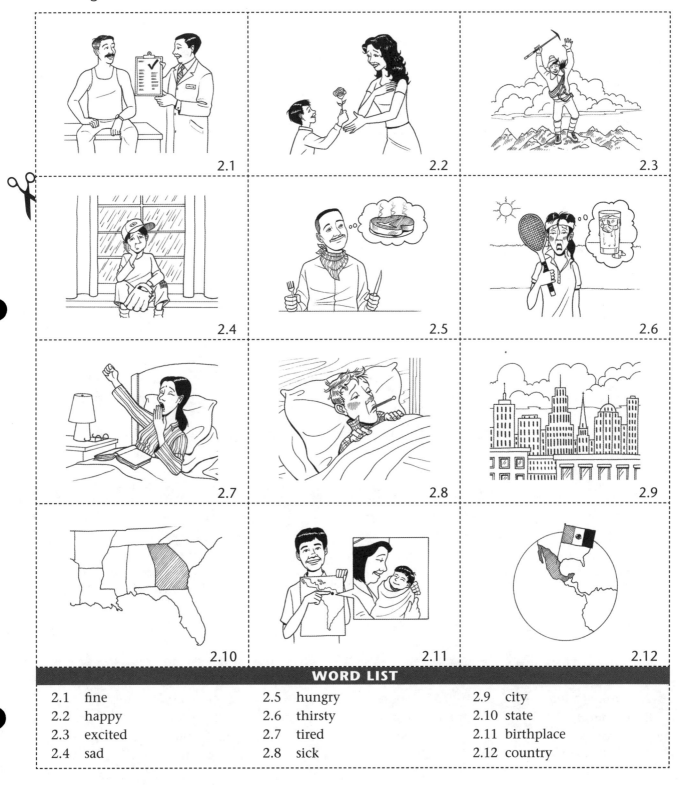

WORD LIST		
2.1 fine	2.5 hungry	2.9 city
2.2 happy	2.6 thirsty	2.10 state
2.3 excited	2.7 tired	2.11 birthplace
2.4 sad	2.8 sick	2.12 country

Picture Cards

1. Cut apart the picture cards. Use the word list to write the words on the back.

2. Work with a partner.

   Partner A: Show the picture card to your partner.

   Partner B: Say the word.

3. Change roles.

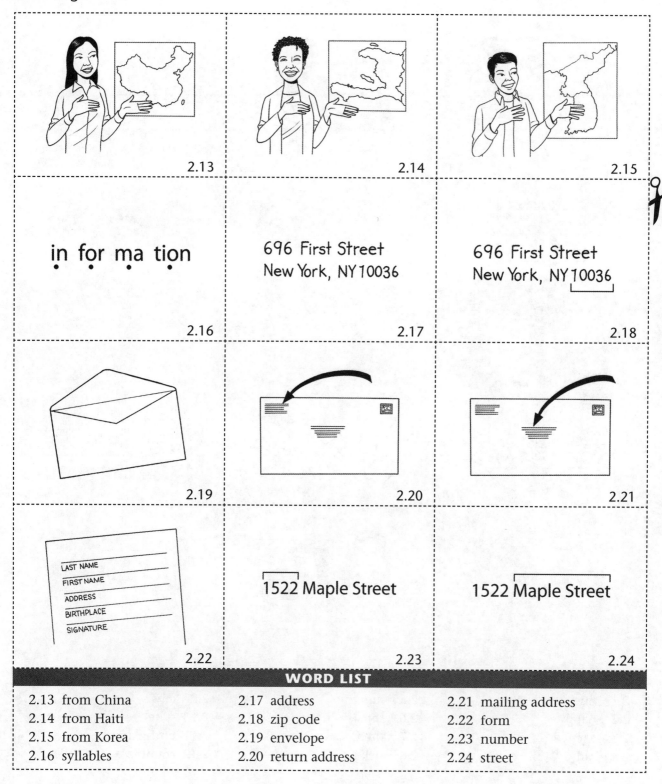

2.13	2.14	2.15
in for ma tion 2.16	696 First Street New York, NY 10036 2.17	696 First Street New York, NY 10036 2.18
2.19	2.20	2.21
LAST NAME FIRST NAME ADDRESS BIRTHPLACE SIGNATURE 2.22	1522 Maple Street 2.23	1522 Maple Street 2.24

WORD LIST		
2.13 from China	2.17 address	2.21 mailing address
2.14 from Haiti	2.18 zip code	2.22 form
2.15 from Korea	2.19 envelope	2.23 number
2.16 syllables	2.20 return address	2.24 street

How Are They Feeling?

1. Work with your classmates.

2. Look at the picture.

3. Say what you see.

4. Watch your teacher write the story on the board or overhead.

5. Copy the story.

_____

_____

_____

_____

_____

_____

_____

_____

About Addresses

Partner A
• **Read a word to Partner B.**   • **Repeat the word.**   • **Watch Partner B write the word.**
1. street   2. city   3. state   4. country
• **Listen to Partner B say a word.**   • **Listen again.**   • **Write the word.**
1.
2.
3.
4.

- - - - - FOLD HERE - - - - -

Partner B
• **Listen to Partner A say a word.**   • **Listen again.**   • **Write the word.**
1.
2.
3.
4.
• **Read a word to Partner A.**   • **Repeat the word.**   • **Watch Partner A write the word.**
1. envelope   2. zip code   3. mailing address   4. return address

Unit 3 What Time Is It?

It's Time for Jim!

1. Work with 3 classmates.

2. Label what you see in the picture.

3. Check your spelling in a dictionary.

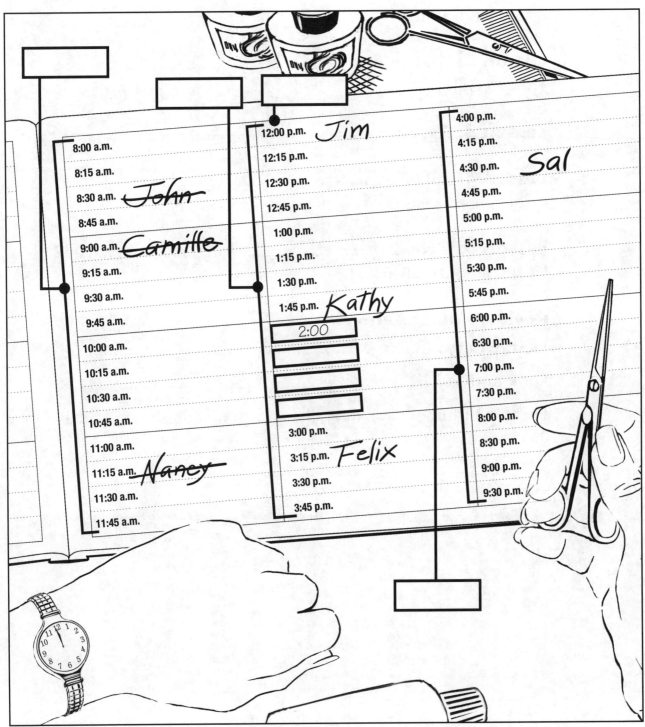

Time to Go!

1. Work with a partner.

2. Read the words in the box.

3. Look at the picture. Circle what you see.

go to the store	go to the library	go to school	~~go to English class~~
go to work	go to the clinic	go home	

4. Look at the picture. Complete the sentences. Use *clinic*, *home*, or *work*.

They go _____ at 7:30 p.m.

They go to _____ at 12:45 p.m.

They go to the _____ at 11:30 a.m.

KEEP GOING!

Work in a group. Write more about the picture.
They go to school at 8:00 a.m.

Sentence Maker

1. Work with a group of 3 or 4 students. Cut apart the cards.

2. Choose a Recorder.

3. Use the word cards to make 5 different sentences or questions in 10 minutes.
The Recorder writes the group's sentences and questions.

YOU	WE	THEY	HE
SHE	IT	ARE	IS
AT	FROM	MEXICO	HOME
SCHOOL	THE	LIBRARY	A
STUDENT	11:00	.	?

Is the Library Open?

1. Work with 2 classmates. Say all the lines in the script.
2. Choose your character.
3. Finish the conversation. Write more lines.
4. Practice the lines.
5. Act out the role-play with your group.

Scene

In a classroom

Characters

- Student 1
- Student 2
- Student 3

Props

- A watch or cell phone
- Notebooks or books

The Script

Student 1: What time is it?

Student 2: It's 10:00 a.m.

Student 1: Is the library open?

Student 2: No, it's not. The library is not open on Saturday morning.

Student 1: Is it open in the afternoon?

Student 3: The library is open at noon.

Student 1: At 12:00?

Student 3: Yes, at 12:00.

Student 1: Is the store open?

KEEP GOING!

Act out the role-play for your class.

How Long Is the Trip?

1. Walk around the room.

2. Ask your classmates: *How long is the trip to* _____?

3. Write the time for the trip.

	Classmate 1	Classmate 2	Classmate 3	Classmate 4
How long is the trip to your home?				
How long is the trip to the store?				
How long is the trip to the clinic?				
How long is the trip to the library?				
How long is the trip to Mexico?				

KEEP GOING!
Talk about this mixer with your class.

Picture Cards

1. Cut apart the picture cards. Use the word list to write the words on the back.
2. Work with a partner.
   Partner A: Show the picture card to your partner.
   Partner B: Say the word.
3. Change roles.

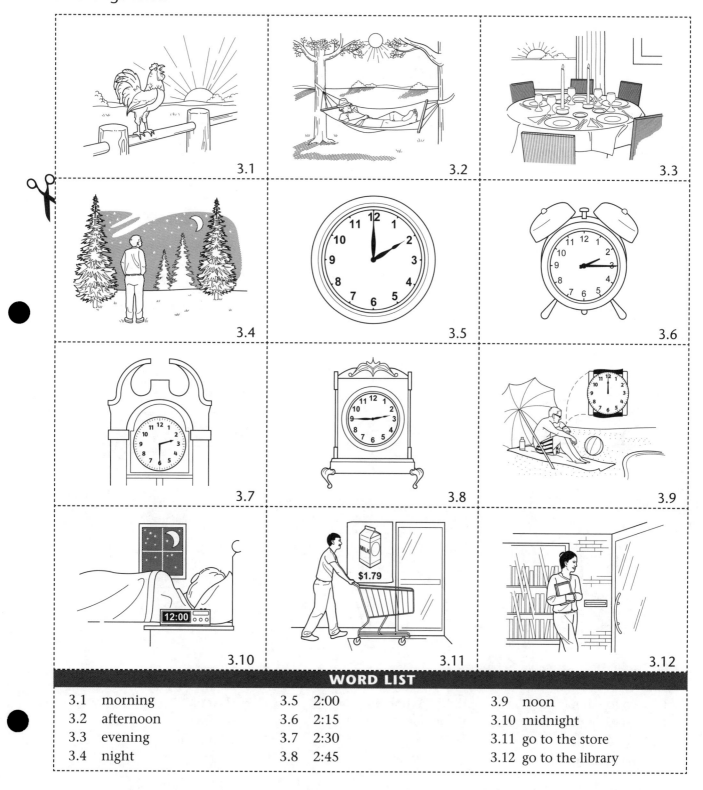

WORD LIST		
3.1 morning	3.5 2:00	3.9 noon
3.2 afternoon	3.6 2:15	3.10 midnight
3.3 evening	3.7 2:30	3.11 go to the store
3.4 night	3.8 2:45	3.12 go to the library

Picture Cards

1. Cut apart the picture cards. Use the word list to write the words on the back.

2. Work with a partner.

    Partner A: Show the picture card to your partner.

    Partner B: Say the word.

3. Change roles.

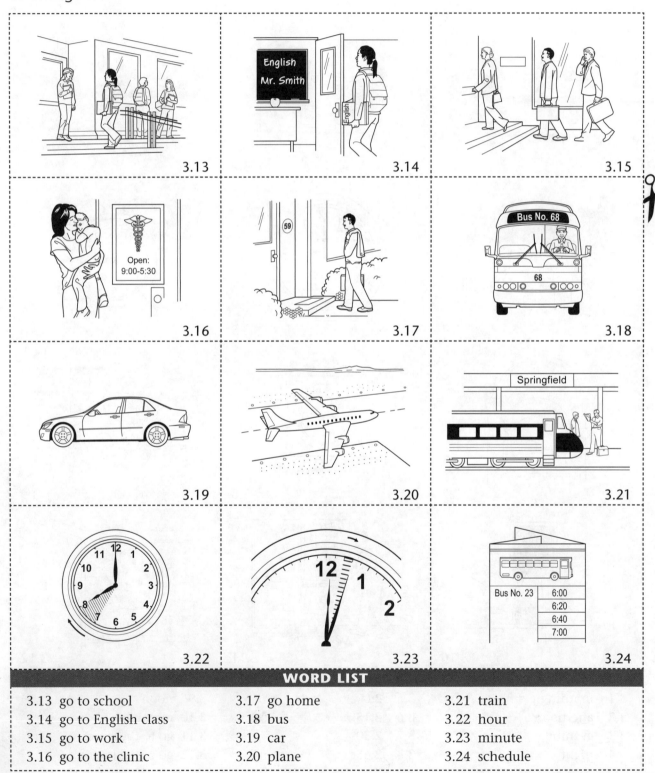

3.13 go to school	3.17 go home	3.21 train
3.14 go to English class	3.18 bus	3.22 hour
3.15 go to work	3.19 car	3.23 minute
3.16 go to the clinic	3.20 plane	3.24 schedule

WORD LIST

They Go to School in the Morning

1. Work with your classmates.

2. Look at the pictures.

3. Say what you see.

4. Watch your teacher write the story on the board or overhead.

5. Copy the story.

_____

_____

_____

_____

_____

_____

_____

It's About Time!

Partner A
• **Read a word to Partner B.** • **Repeat the word.** • **Watch Partner B write the word.**
1. morning 2. afternoon 3. evening 4. night
• **Listen to Partner B say a word.** • **Listen again.** • **Write the word.**
1.
2.
3.
4.

- - - - - - - - - - - - - - - - - - FOLD HERE - - - - - - - - - - - - - - - - - -

Partner B
• **Listen to Partner A say a word.** • **Listen again.** • **Write the word.**
1.
2.
3.
4.
• **Read a word to Partner A.** • **Repeat the word.** • **Watch Partner A write the word.**
1. trip 2. minute 3. hour 4. schedule

Unit 4 What Day Is It?

In One Week

1. Work with 3 classmates.

2. Label what you see in the picture.

3. Check your spelling in a dictionary.

KEEP GOING!

Talk about the picture. Say what you see.

My Next Birthday

1. Work with a partner.

2. Read the words in the box.

3. Look at the picture. Circle what you see.

January	February	March	April	May	June	~~month~~	year

4. Look at the picture. Complete the sentences. Use *month, year,* or *April*.

It's _____.

Next _____ is May.

Next _____ is 2010.

KEEP GOING!

Work in a group. Write more about the picture.
Today is Thursday.

Sentence Maker

1. Work with a group of 3 or 4 students. Cut apart the cards.
2. Choose a Recorder.
3. Use the word cards to make 5 different sentences or questions in 10 minutes.
   The Recorder writes the group's sentences and questions.

THE	BIRTHDAY	CLASS	PARTY
IS	ON	AT	FRIDAY
SATURDAY	7:30	5:00	MY
HOUSE	SCHOOL	WHEN	WHERE
WHAT	TIME	.	?

When Is the Party?

1. Work with 2 classmates. Say all the lines in the script.

2. Choose your character.

3. Finish the conversation. Write more lines.

4. Practice the lines.

5. Act out the role-play with your group.

Scene	**Characters**	**Props**
At the library	• Vic • Shawn • Sam	• Books and/or notebooks • A piece of paper or invitation

The Script

Vic: Goodbye, Sam. Have a nice weekend.

Shawn: Weekend? Today is not Friday.

Vic: It's not?

Sam: No, it's not. Tomorrow is Friday.

Vic: Oh, yes. Today is Thursday.

Sam: The birthday party for Mona is this weekend.

Vic: When is the party?

Shawn: Look at the invitation.

KEEP GOING!

Act out the role-play for your class.

When Is Your Birthday?

1. Walk around the room.
2. Ask your classmates: *When is your birthday?*
3. Write the names and birthdays of your classmates.

	Name	Birthday
Classmate 1		
Classmate 2		
Classmate 3		
Classmate 4		
Classmate 5		
Classmate 6		
Classmate 7		
Classmate 8		
Classmate 9		
Classmate 10		

KEEP GOING!
Talk about this mixer with your class.

Picture Cards

1. Cut apart the picture cards. Use the word list to write the words on the back.

2. Work with a partner.

   Partner A: Show the picture card to your partner.

   Partner B: Say the word.

3. Change roles.

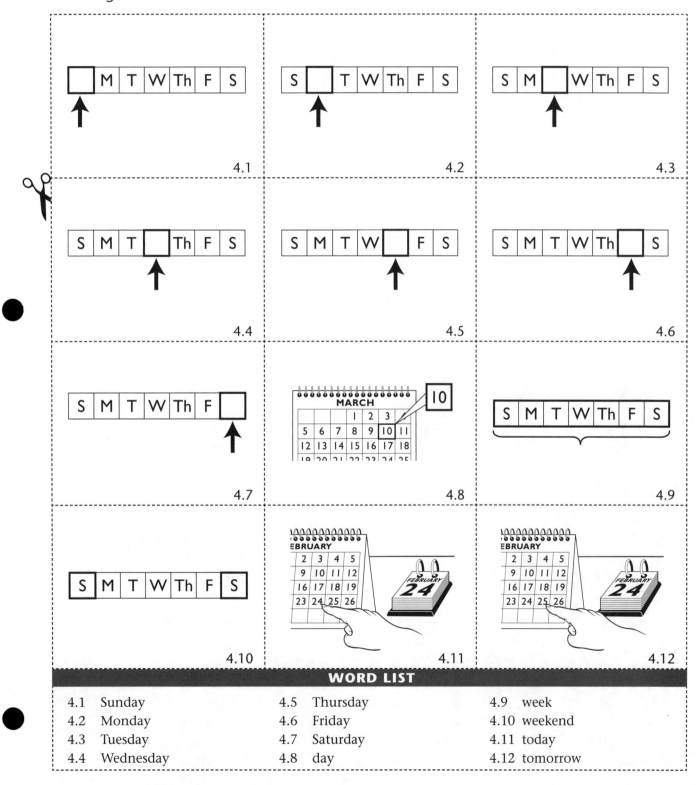

WORD LIST		
4.1 Sunday	4.5 Thursday	4.9 week
4.2 Monday	4.6 Friday	4.10 weekend
4.3 Tuesday	4.7 Saturday	4.11 today
4.4 Wednesday	4.8 day	4.12 tomorrow

Picture Cards

1. Cut apart the picture cards. Use the word list to write the words on the back.
2. Work with a partner.
   Partner A: Show the picture card to your partner.
   Partner B: Say the word.
3. Change roles.

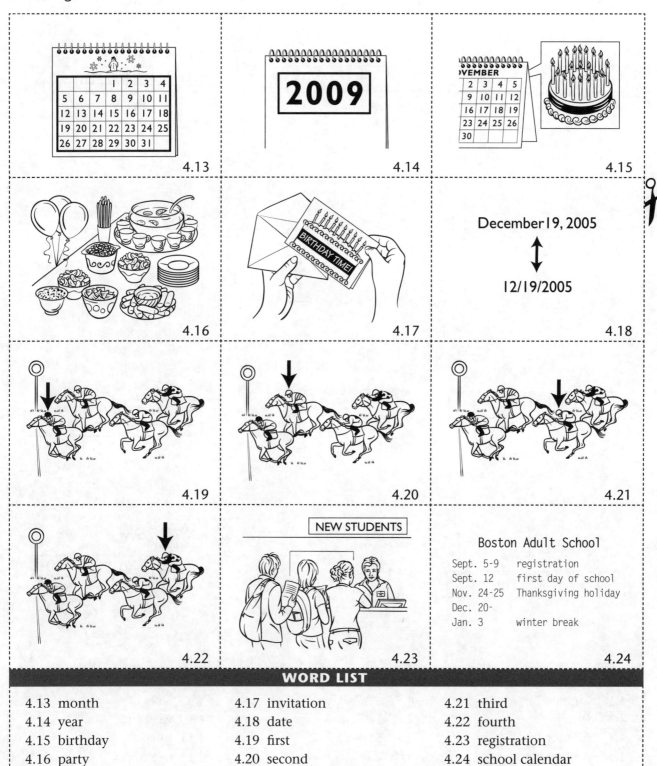

4.13	4.14	4.15
4.16	4.17	4.18
4.19	4.20	4.21
4.22	4.23	4.24

WORD LIST

4.13 month	4.17 invitation	4.21 third
4.14 year	4.18 date	4.22 fourth
4.15 birthday	4.19 first	4.23 registration
4.16 party	4.20 second	4.24 school calendar

When Is Registration?

1. Work with your classmates.

2. Look at the picture.

3. Say what you see.

4. Watch your teacher write the story on the board or overhead.

City Adult School

5870 Broad Street
Los Angeles, CA 90036

IMPORTANT DATES AND INFORMATION

September 1–5 .... registration
September 9 .... the first day of school
November 26–27 .... Thanksgiving holiday
December 18–January 6 .... winter break
June 25 .... the last day of school
June 26 .... school party (4:00 p.m. at Pizza City)

The school library is open from 8:00 a.m. to 8:00 p.m.

The school store is open from 10:00 a.m. to 6:00 p.m.

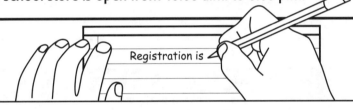

Registration is

5. Copy the story.

_____

_____

_____

_____

_____

_____

_____

On the Calendar

Partner A
• **Read a word to Partner B.** • **Repeat the word.** • **Watch Partner B write the word.**
1. today 2. Tuesday 3. February 4. twenty-fifth
• **Listen to Partner B say a word.** • **Listen again.** • **Write the word.**
1.
2.
3.
4.

- - - - - - - - - - - - - - - FOLD HERE - - - - - - - - - - - - - - -

Partner B
• **Listen to Partner A say a word.** • **Listen again.** • **Write the word.**
1.
2.
3.
4.
• **Read a word to Partner A.** • **Repeat the word.** • **Watch Partner A write the word.**
1. tomorrow 2. Thursday 3. December 4. eighteenth

Unit 5 How Much Is It?

Dollars and Cents

1. Work with 3 classmates.

2. Label what you see in the picture.

3. Check your spelling in a dictionary.

KEEP GOING!

Talk about the picture. Say what you see.

Shopping for Clothes

1. Work with a partner.
2. Read the words in the box.
3. Look at the picture. Circle what you see.

shirt	price	sweater	pants	socks	shoes	~~cheap~~	expensive

4. Look at the picture. Complete the sentences. Use *expensive, cheap,* or *store.*

They are at the _____.

The sweaters are _____.

The shirts are _____.

KEEP GOING!
Work in a group. Write more about the picture.
They are shopping.

Sentence Maker

1. Work with a group of 3 or 4 students. Cut apart the cards.

2. Choose a Recorder.

3. Use the word cards to make 5 different sentences in 10 minutes.
The Recorder writes the group's sentences.

THIS	THAT	THESE	THOSE
SHIRT	SWEATER	STORE	CLOTHES
PANTS	SOCKS	SHOES	PENS
PENCIL	IS	ARE	EXPENSIVE
CHEAP	$60.15	$15.90	.

That's Expensive!

1. Work with 2 classmates. Say all the lines in the script.
2. Choose your character.
3. Finish the conversation. Write more lines.
4. Practice the lines.
5. Act out the role-play with your group.

Scene	Characters	Props
At a clothing store	• Kam • Chris • Lu	2 sweaters

The Script

Kam: Chris, look at this sweater.

Chris: That's nice!

Lu: How much is it?

Kam: It's $38.50.

Lu: That's expensive!

Chris: No it's not. That's cheap for a nice sweater.

Lu: It's expensive to me!

Chris: Look at this sweater.

Lu: That's a nice sweater, too!

Kam: How much is it?

KEEP GOING!
Act out the role-play for your class.

Cheap or Expensive?

1. Walk around the room.

2. Ask your classmates: *Is your _____ cheap or expensive?*

3. Write your classmates' names and answers in the boxes.

Classmates' Names	Is your electric bill cheap or expensive?	Is your gas bill cheap or expensive?
Classmate 1:		
Classmate 2:		
Classmate 3:		
Classmate 4:		
Classmate 5:		
Classmate 6:		
Classmate 7:		
Classmate 8:		
Classmate 9:		
Classmate 10:		

KEEP GOING!

Talk about this mixer with your class.

Picture Cards

1. Cut apart the picture cards. Use the word list to write the words on the back.

2. Work with a partner.

    Partner A: Show the picture card to your partner.

    Partner B: Say the word.

3. Change roles.

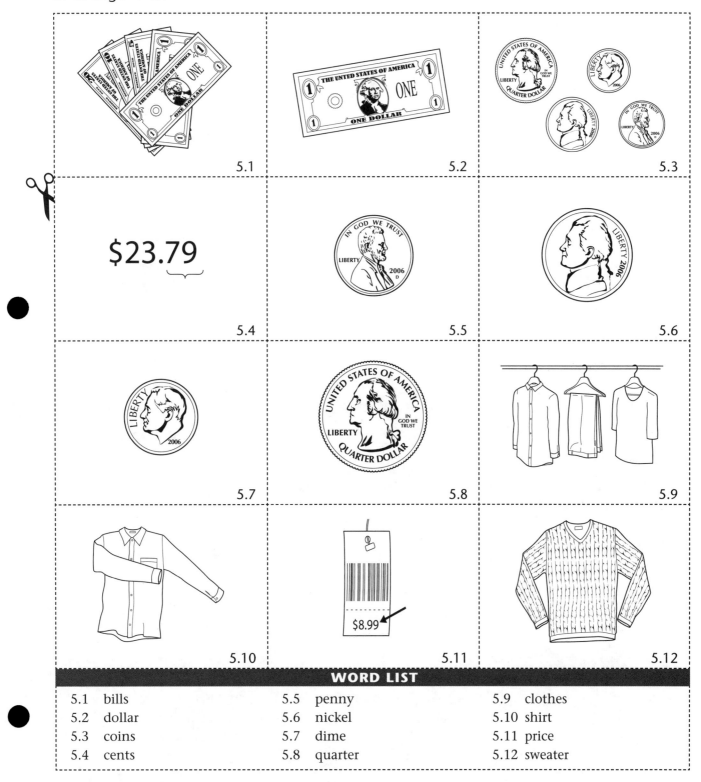

WORD LIST		
5.1 bills	5.5 penny	5.9 clothes
5.2 dollar	5.6 nickel	5.10 shirt
5.3 coins	5.7 dime	5.11 price
5.4 cents	5.8 quarter	5.12 sweater

Picture Cards

1. Cut apart the picture cards. Use the word list to write the words on the back.

2. Work with a partner.

    Partner A: Show the picture card to your partner.

    Partner B: Say the word.

3. Change roles.

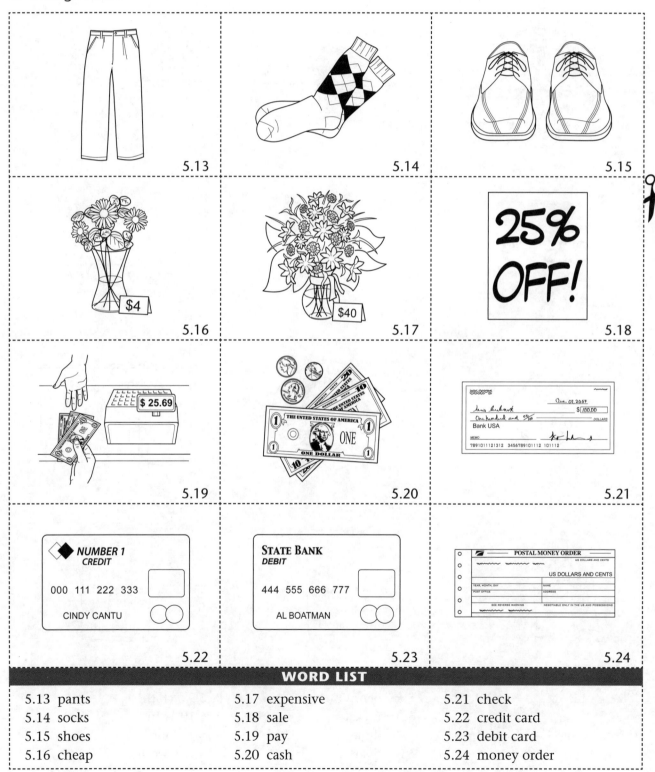

5.13

5.14

5.15

5.16

5.17

5.18

5.19

5.20

5.21

5.22

5.23

5.24

WORD LIST		
5.13 pants	5.17 expensive	5.21 check
5.14 socks	5.18 sale	5.22 credit card
5.15 shoes	5.19 pay	5.23 debit card
5.16 cheap	5.20 cash	5.24 money order

Those Shirts Are 50% Off!

1. Work with your classmates.

2. Look at the picture.

3. Say what you see.

4. Watch your teacher write the story on the board or overhead.

5. Copy the story.

_____

_____

_____

_____

_____

_____

_____

This and That

Partner A
• **Read a word to Partner B.** • **Repeat the word.** • **Watch Partner B write the word.**
1. this 2. shirt 3. these 4. shoes
• **Listen to Partner B say a word.** • **Listen again.** • **Write the word.**
1.
2.
3.
4.

- FOLD HERE -

Partner B
• **Listen to Partner A say a word.** • **Listen again.** • **Write the word.**
1.
2.
3.
4.
• **Read a word to Partner A.** • **Repeat the word.** • **Watch Partner A write the word.**
1. that 2. sweater 3. those 4. pants

Unit 6 That's My Son

These Are My Parents

1. Work with 3 classmates.

2. Label what you see in the picture.

3. Check your spelling in a dictionary.

father

KEEP GOING!

Talk about the picture. Say what you see.

Happy Birthday!

1. Work with a partner.

2. Read the words in the box.

3. Look at the picture. Circle what you see.

children	~~child~~	daughter	son	brother	sister

4. Look at the picture. Complete the sentences. Use *children, sister,* or *brother.*

Mary is the _____.

The _____ are at a birthday party.

Gary is the _____.

KEEP GOING!

Work in a group. Write more about the picture.
The child is hungry.

Sentence Maker

1. Work with a group of 3 or 4 students. Cut apart the cards.

2. Choose a Recorder.

3. Use the word cards to make 5 different sentences in 10 minutes.
     The Recorder writes the group's sentences.

HIS	HER	YOUR	NAME
NAMES	IS	ARE	MEL
AND	ALI	HE	SHE
THEY	LIVE	LIVES	IN
NEW YORK	CALIFORNIA	.	YOUR

Who's That?

1. Work with 2 classmates. Say all the lines in the script.

2. Choose your character.

3. Finish the conversation. Write more lines.

4. Practice the lines.

5. Act out the role-play with your group.

Scene

At a house

Characters

- Kim
- Toni
- Rene

Props

A photograph

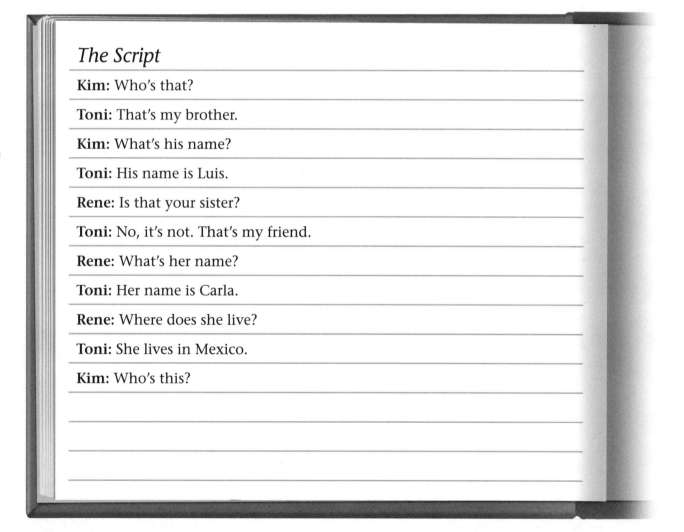

The Script

Kim: Who's that?

Toni: That's my brother.

Kim: What's his name?

Toni: His name is Luis.

Rene: Is that your sister?

Toni: No, it's not. That's my friend.

Rene: What's her name?

Toni: Her name is Carla.

Rene: Where does she live?

Toni: She lives in Mexico.

Kim: Who's this?

KEEP GOING!

Act out the role-play for your class.

Do You Come to Class Every Day?

1. Walk around the room.

2. Ask your classmates: *Do you* _____?

3. Write *yes* or *no* in the boxes for your classmates.

	Classmate 1	Classmate 2	Classmate 3	Classmate 4	Classmate 5
Do you come to class every day?					
Do you come to class on time?					
Do you do your homework?					

KEEP GOING!

Talk about this mixer with your class.

Picture Cards

1. Cut apart the picture cards. Use the word list to write the words on the back.

2. Work with a partner.

    Partner A: Show the picture card to your partner.

    Partner B: Say the word.

3. Change roles.

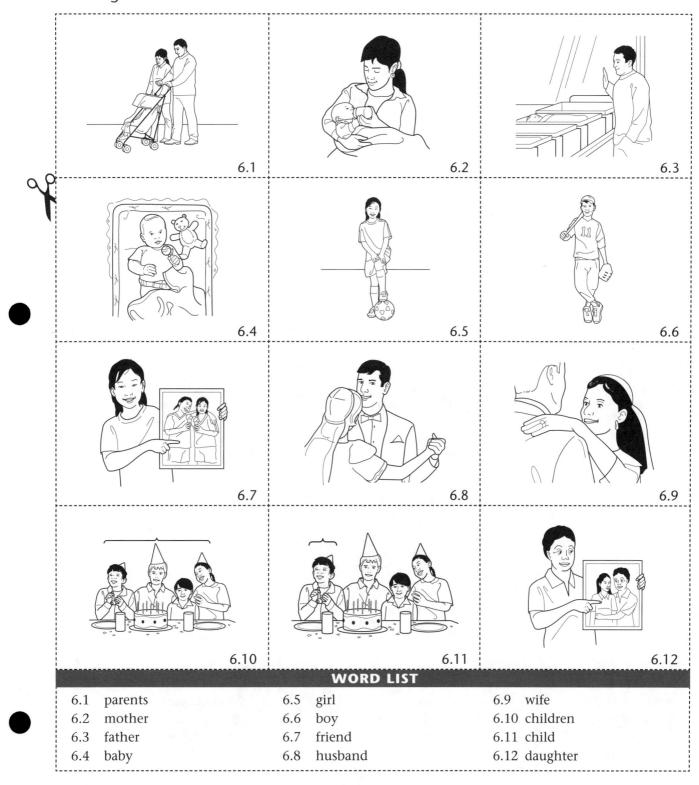

WORD LIST		
6.1 parents	6.5 girl	6.9 wife
6.2 mother	6.6 boy	6.10 children
6.3 father	6.7 friend	6.11 child
6.4 baby	6.8 husband	6.12 daughter

Picture Cards

1. Cut apart the picture cards. Use the word list to write the words on the back.

2. Work with a partner.

   Partner A: Show the picture card to your partner.

   Partner B: Say the word.

3. Change roles.

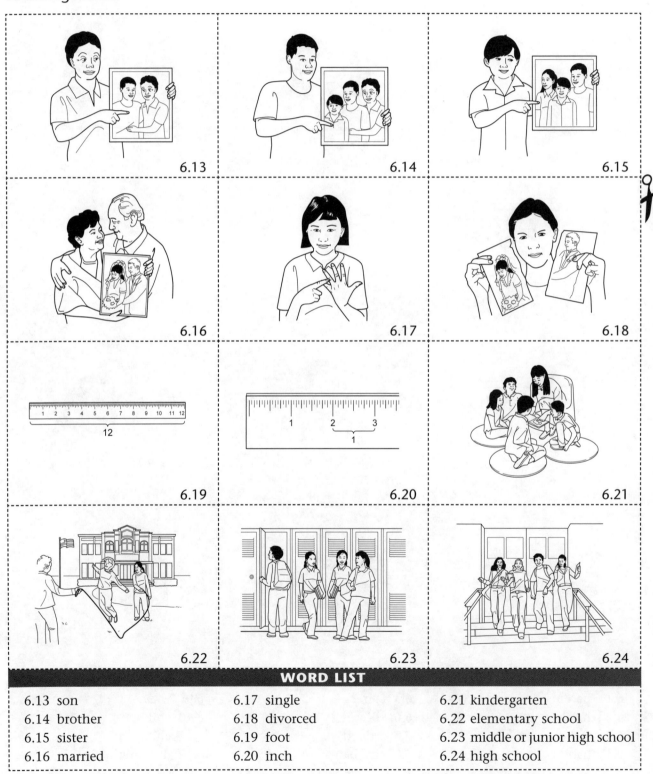

WORD LIST		
6.13 son	6.17 single	6.21 kindergarten
6.14 brother	6.18 divorced	6.22 elementary school
6.15 sister	6.19 foot	6.23 middle or junior high school
6.16 married	6.20 inch	6.24 high school

The Flores Family

1. Work with your classmates.

2. Look at the picture.

3. Say what you see.

4. Watch your teacher write the story on the board or overhead.

The Flores Family

Alberto Flores, 41 years old,
Teacher, Elm High School.

Lorena Flores, 36 years old,
Student, Montoya Adult School.

Nancy Flores, 13 years old,
Student, Newport Junior High School.

Jim Flores, 15 years old,
Student, City High School.

David Flores, 11 years old,
Student, Brook Street Elementary School.

---

5. Copy the story.

_____

_____

_____

_____

_____

_____

_____

In the Family

Partner A
• **Read a word to Partner B.** • **Repeat the word.** • **Watch Partner B write the word.**
1. mother 2. sister 3. wife 4. daughter
• **Listen to Partner B say a word.** • **Listen again.** • **Write the word.**
1.
2.
3.
4.

- - - - - - - - - - - - - - - - - FOLD HERE - - - - - - - - - - - - - - - -

Partner B
• **Listen to Partner A say a word.** • **Listen again.** • **Write the word.**
1.
2.
3.
4.
• **Read a word to Partner A.** • **Repeat the word.** • **Watch Partner A write the word.**
1. father 2. brother 3. husband 4. son

Unit 7 Do We Need Apples?

Fruits and Vegetables

1. Work with 3 classmates.

2. Label what you see in the picture.

3. Check your spelling in a dictionary.

fruit

KEEP GOING!

Talk about the picture. Say what you see.

At the Supermarket

1. Work with a partner.

2. Read the words in the box.

3. Look at the picture. Circle what you see.

| cheese | eggs | ~~milk~~ | bread | pork | chicken | lamb | beef |

4. Look at the picture. Complete the sentences. Use *cheese, eggs,* or *beef.*

The mother likes _____.

The daughter likes _____.

The husband likes _____.

KEEP GOING!

Work in a group. Write more about the picture.
They buy bread.

Sentence Maker

1. Work with a group of 3 or 4 students. Cut apart the cards.

2. Choose a Recorder.

3. Use the word cards to make 5 different sentences or questions in 10 minutes.
The Recorder writes the group's sentences and questions.

I	YOU	HE	SHE
WE	THEY	LIKE	LIKES
NEED	DOES	DO	DOESN'T
DON'T	BROCCOLI	EGGS	MILK
BREAD	RICE	.	?

Ask the Clerk

1. Work with 2 classmates. Say all the lines in the script.

2. Choose your character.

3. Finish the conversation. Write more lines for the characters.

4. Practice the lines.

5. Act out the role-play with your group.

Scene	**Characters**	**Props**
At a store	• Friend 1 • Friend 2 • Clerk	A shopping list or piece of paper

The Script

Friend 1: We need milk.

Friend 2: I don't see the milk.

Friend 1: Ask the clerk.

Friend 2: Excuse me. Where is the milk?

Clerk: Here you go.

Friend 2: Thank you.

Clerk: You're welcome.

Friend 2: Do we need rice?

Friend 1: No. We need corn.

Friend 2: Oh. Do you see the vegetables?

Friend 1: No, I don't. Ask the clerk.

KEEP GOING!

Act out the role-play for your class.

What Do You Buy?

1. Walk around the room.

2. Ask your classmates: *Do you buy* _____ *at the supermarket?*

3. Write *yes* or *no* for your classmates.

	Classmate 1	Classmate 2	Classmate 3
Do you buy fruit at the supermarket?			
Do you buy cheese at the supermarket?			
Do you buy cabbage at the supermarket?			
Do you buy coffee at the supermarket?			
Do you buy tea at the supermarket?			
Do you buy water at the supermarket?			

KEEP GOING!

Talk about this mixer with your class.

Picture Cards

1. Cut apart the picture cards. Use the word list to write the words on the back.
2. Work with a partner.
   Partner A: Show the picture card to your partner.
   Partner B: Say the word.
3. Change roles.

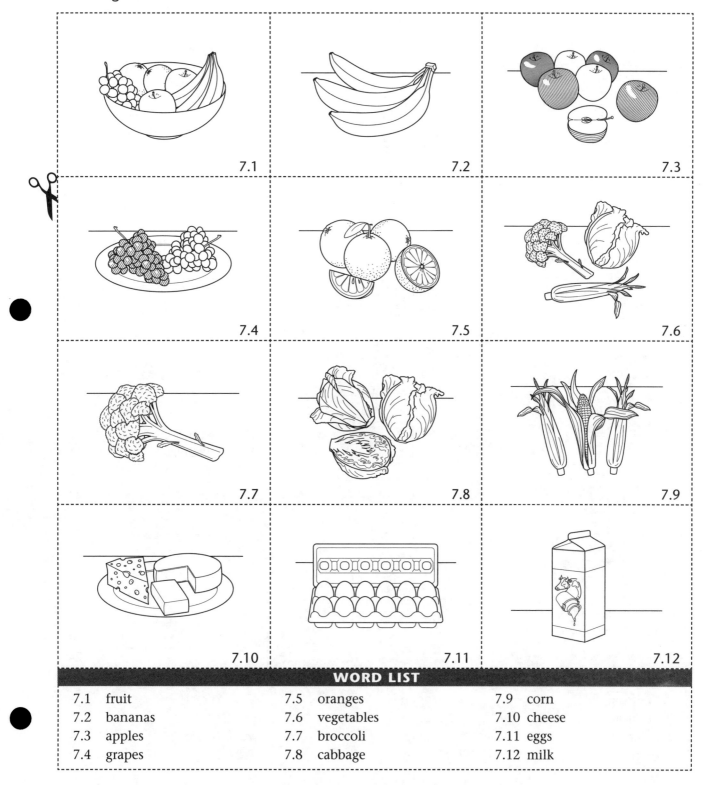

7.1	7.2	7.3
7.4	7.5	7.6
7.7	7.8	7.9
7.10	7.11	7.12

WORD LIST

7.1	fruit	7.5	oranges	7.9	corn
7.2	bananas	7.6	vegetables	7.10	cheese
7.3	apples	7.7	broccoli	7.11	eggs
7.4	grapes	7.8	cabbage	7.12	milk

Picture Cards

1. Cut apart the picture cards. Use the word list to write the words on the back.

2. Work with a partner.

   Partner A: Show the picture card to your partner.

   Partner B: Say the word.

3. Change roles.

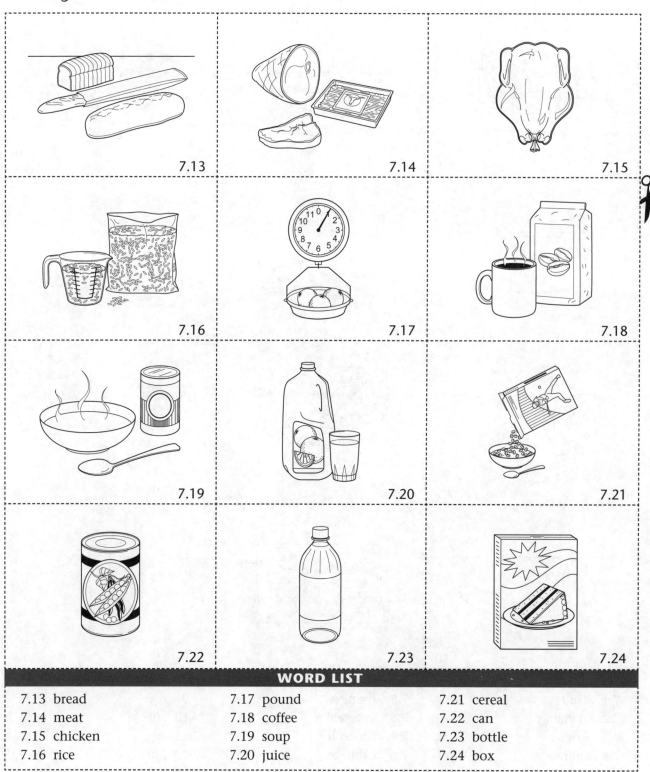

	WORD LIST	
7.13 bread	7.17 pound	7.21 cereal
7.14 meat	7.18 coffee	7.22 can
7.15 chicken	7.19 soup	7.23 bottle
7.16 rice	7.20 juice	7.24 box

They Like Shopping!

1. Work with your classmates.

2. Look at the picture.

3. Say what you see.

4. Watch your teacher write the story on the board or overhead.

5. Copy the story.

_____

_____

_____

_____

_____

_____

_____

_____

What Do You Like?

Partner A
• **Read a sentence to Partner B.** • **Repeat the sentence.** • **Watch Partner B complete the sentence.**
1. My friends like meat. 2. Alberto likes beef. 3. Gloria likes lamb. 4. They don't like cheese.
• **Listen to Partner B say a sentence.** • **Listen again.** • **Complete the sentence.**
5. Sharon _____ bananas.
6. I like _____.
7. We like _____, too.
8. Do you like _____?

- - - - - - - - - - - - - - - - - - FOLD HERE -

Partner B
• **Listen to Partner A say a sentence.** • **Listen again.** • **Complete the sentence.**
1. My friends like _____.
2. Alberto likes _____.
3. Gloria likes _____.
4. They don't like _____.
• **Read a sentence to Partner A.** • **Repeat the sentence.** • **Watch Partner A complete the sentence.**
5. Sharon likes bananas. 6. I like apples. 7. We like grapes, too. 8. Do you like fruit?

Unit 8 Take Two Tablets

Parts of the Body

1. Work with 3 classmates.

2. Label what you see in the picture.

3. Check your spelling in a dictionary.

head

KEEP GOING!

Talk about the picture. Say what you see.

They're All Sick

1. Work with a partner.

2. Read the words in the box.

3. Look at the picture. Circle what you see.

a cold	an earache	a sore throat	a headache
a stomachache	a fever	a cough	~~the flu~~

4. Look at the picture. Complete the sentences. Use *cold, headache,* or *sore throat*.

Mona has a _____.

Oscar has a _____.

Zita has a _____.

> **KEEP GOING!**
>
> Work in a group. Write more about the picture.
> *Ivan has a stomachache.*

Sentence Maker

1. Work with a group of 3 or 4 students. Cut apart the cards.

2. Choose a Recorder.

3. Use the word cards to make 5 different sentences or questions in 10 minutes.
The Recorder writes the group's sentences and questions.

I	YOU	WE	THEY
HE	SHE	HAVE	HAS
DO	DOES	A	AN
COLD	HEADACHES	STOMACHACHE	EARACHE
FEVER	SORE THROATS	.	?

What's the Matter?

1. Work with 2 classmates. Say all the lines in the script.
2. Choose your character.
3. Finish the conversation. Write more lines for the characters.
4. Practice the lines.
5. Act out the role-play with your group.

Scene

A telephone
conversation

Characters

- Receptionist
- Lee Jones
- Doctor

Props

Two telephones

The Script

Receptionist: Hello, City Clinic.

Lee: This is Lee Jones. I need to see the doctor today.

Receptionist: What's the matter?

Lee: I have an earache.

Receptionist: One minute, please. Doctor, Lee Jones needs to see you today.

Doctor: What's the matter?

Receptionist: He has an earache.

Doctor: Does he have a fever?

Receptionist: Hello, Lee. Do you have a fever?

Lee: Yes, I do.

Receptionist: Is 4:00 OK?

KEEP GOING!
Act out the role-play for your class.

When I'm Sick...

1. Walk around the room.

2. Ask your classmates to complete the sentence: *When I'm sick, _____.*

3. Write a check in the boxes for your classmates.

	Classmate 1	Classmate 2	Classmate 3	Classmate 4	Classmate 5
When I'm sick, I see the doctor.					
When I'm sick, I don't go to school.					
When I'm sick, I take medicine.					
When I'm sick, I have juice and water.					
When I'm sick, I eat chicken soup.					

KEEP GOING!
Talk about this mixer with your class.

Picture Cards

1. Cut apart the picture cards. Use the word list to write the words on the back.

2. Work with a partner.

    Partner A: Show the picture card to your partner.

    Partner B: Say the word.

3. Change roles.

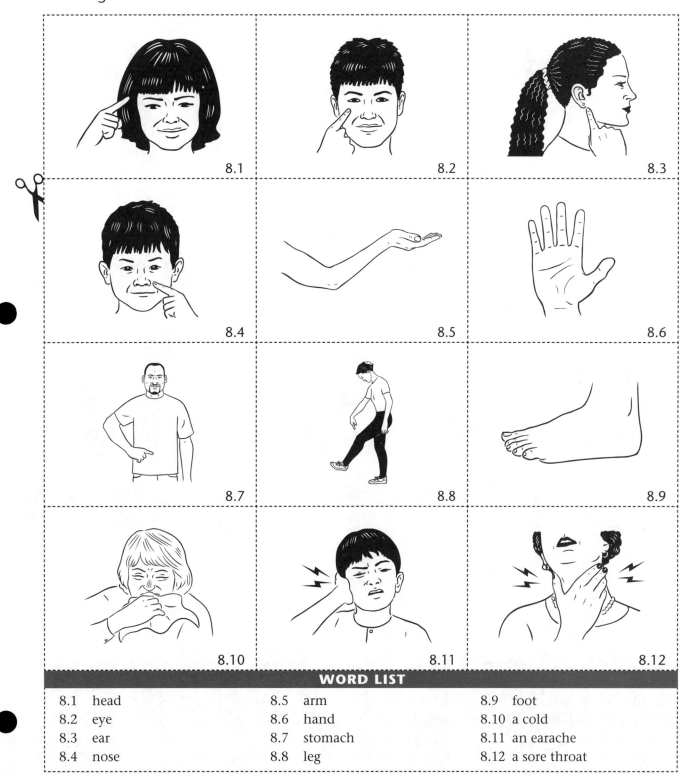

WORD LIST		
8.1 head	8.5 arm	8.9 foot
8.2 eye	8.6 hand	8.10 a cold
8.3 ear	8.7 stomach	8.11 an earache
8.4 nose	8.8 leg	8.12 a sore throat

Picture Cards

1. Cut apart the picture cards. Use the word list to write the words on the back.

2. Work with a partner.

Partner A: Show the picture card to your partner.

Partner B: Say the word.

3. Change roles.

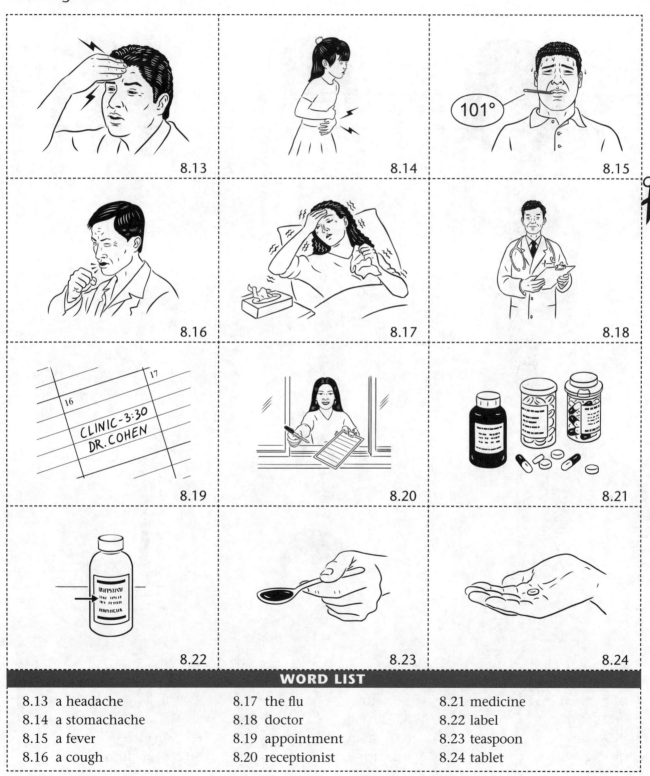

8.13

8.14

8.15

8.16

8.17

8.18

8.19

8.20

8.21

8.22

8.23

8.24

WORD LIST		
8.13 a headache	8.17 the flu	8.21 medicine
8.14 a stomachache	8.18 doctor	8.22 label
8.15 a fever	8.19 appointment	8.23 teaspoon
8.16 a cough	8.20 receptionist	8.24 tablet

Lily Is Sick

1. Work with your classmates.

2. Look at the picture.

3. Say what you see.

4. Watch your teacher write the story on the board or overhead.

5. Copy the story.

_____

_____

_____

_____

_____

_____

See the Doctor

Partner A
• **Read a sentence to Partner B.** • **Repeat the sentence.** • **Watch Partner B complete the sentence.**
1. Does Tom have a sore throat? 2. Yes, he does. 3. He has an earache, too. 4. He needs to see the doctor.
• **Listen to Partner B say a sentence.** • **Listen again.** • **Complete the sentence.**
5. Do the children have _____?
6. Yes, _____ do.
7. They don't have _____.
8. They have the _____.

- FOLD HERE -

Partner B
• **Listen to Partner A say a sentence.** • **Listen again.** • **Complete the sentence.**
1. Does Tom have a sore _____?
2. Yes, _____ does.
3. He has an _____, too.
4. He needs to see the _____.
• **Read a sentence to Partner A.** • **Repeat the sentence.** • **Watch Partner A complete the sentence.**
5. Do the children have fevers? 6. Yes, they do. 7. They don't have stomachaches. 8. They have the flu.

Unit 9 What Size?

What Color Is Correct?

1. Work with 3 classmates.

2. Label the correct color of the things in the picture.

3. Check your spelling in a dictionary.

KEEP GOING!

Talk about the picture. Say what you see.

Nice Clothes!

1. Work with a partner.

2. Read the words in the box.

3. Look at the picture. Circle what you see.

shorts	T-shirt	cap	~~jacket~~	dress	coat	belt	boots

4. Look at the picture. Complete the sentences. Use *dress, cap,* or *T-shirt*.

The _____ is $7.00.

She's wearing a white _____.

She's wearing a black _____.

> **KEEP GOING!**
>
> Work in a group. Write more about the picture.
> *The store sells clothes.*

Sentence Maker

1. Work with a group of 3 or 4 students. Cut apart the cards.

2. Choose a Recorder.

3. Use the word cards to make 5 different sentences or questions in 10 minutes.
   The Recorder writes the group's sentences and questions.

I	YOU	WE	THEY
HE	SHE	AM	ARE
IS	WEARING	READING	A
WHITE	RED	BOOK	CAP
T-SHIRT	SHOES	.	?

What Size?

1. Work with 2 classmates. Say all the lines in the script.

2. Choose your character.

3. Finish the conversation. Write more lines for the characters.

4. Practice the lines.

5. Act out the role-play with your group.

Scene	**Characters**	**Props**
A clothing store	• Friend 1 • Clerk • Friend 2	• A jacket • A sweater

The Script

Friend 1: Excuse me. I'm looking for a jacket.

Clerk: What size?

Friend 1: I need a large.

Friend 2: No, you don't. You need a medium.

Clerk: OK. Here's a medium.

Friend 1: Thank you.

Clerk: Are you looking for a jacket, too?

Friend 2: No, I'm not. I'm looking for a sweater.

Clerk: What size?

KEEP GOING!

Act out the role-play for your class.

I'm Wearing Red Shoes

1. Walk around the room.

2. Tell your classmates to complete the sentence: *I'm wearing* _____ *shoes.*

3. Write your classmates' names and the colors.

Classmates' Names	I'm wearing _____ shoes.

KEEP GOING!

Talk about this mixer with your class.

Picture Cards

1. Cut apart the picture cards. Use the word list to write the words on the back.

2. Work with a partner.

Partner A: Show the picture card to your partner.

Partner B: Say the word.

3. Change roles.

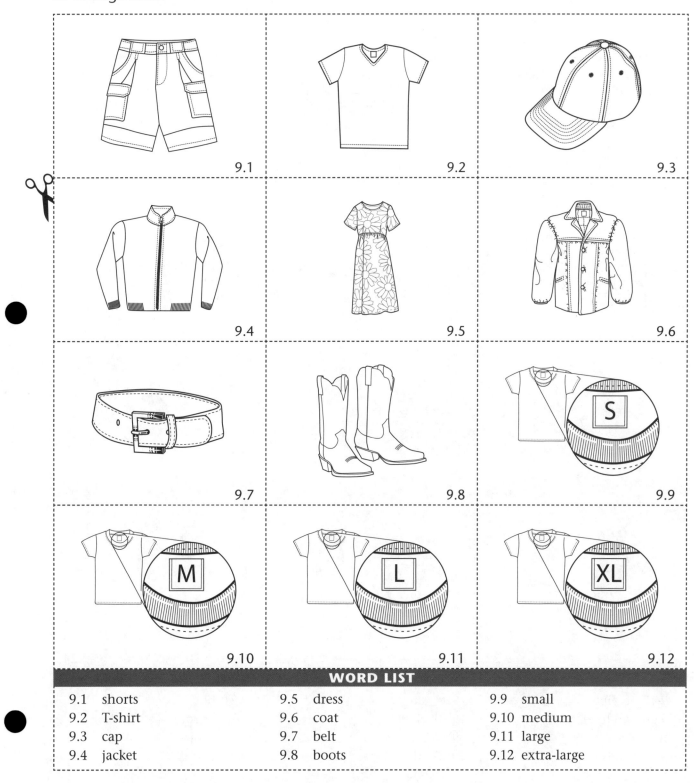

9.1

9.2

9.3

9.4

9.5

9.6

9.7

9.8

9.9

9.10

9.11

9.12

WORD LIST		
9.1 shorts	9.5 dress	9.9 small
9.2 T-shirt	9.6 coat	9.10 medium
9.3 cap	9.7 belt	9.11 large
9.4 jacket	9.8 boots	9.12 extra-large

Picture Cards

1. Cut apart the picture cards. Use the word list to write the words on the back.

2. Work with a partner.

   Partner A: Show the picture card to your partner.

   Partner B: Say the word.

3. Change roles.

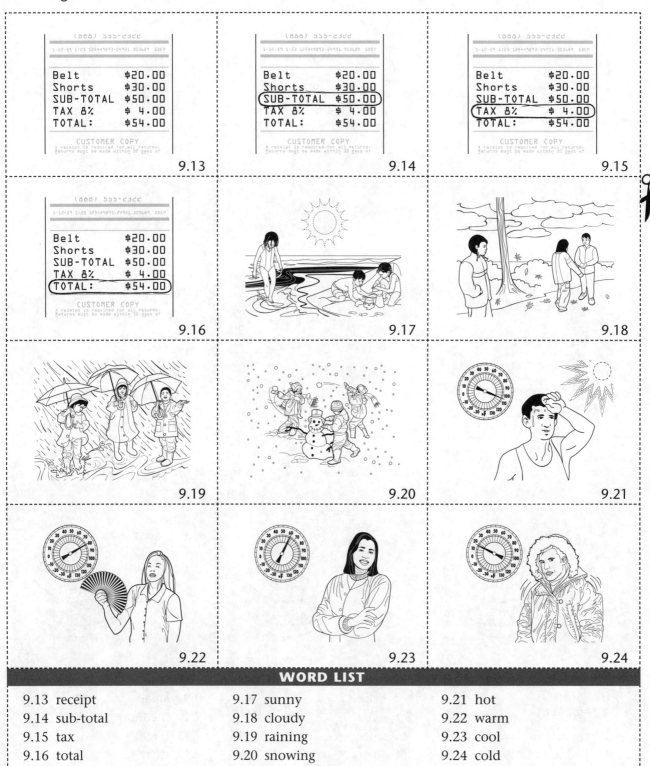

WORD LIST		
9.13 receipt	9.17 sunny	9.21 hot
9.14 sub-total	9.18 cloudy	9.22 warm
9.15 tax	9.19 raining	9.23 cool
9.16 total	9.20 snowing	9.24 cold

How Is the Weather?

1. Work with your classmates.

2. Look at the picture.

3. Say what you see.

4. Watch your teacher write the story on the board or overhead.

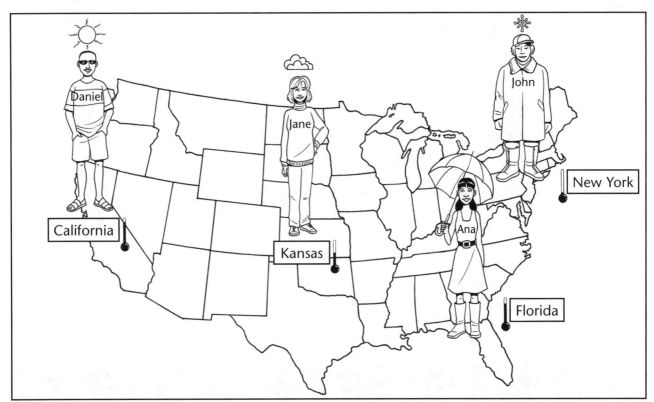

5. Copy the story.

_____

_____

_____

_____

_____

_____

_____

What Are They Wearing?

Partner A
• **Read a sentence to Partner B.** • **Repeat the sentence.** • **Watch Partner B complete the sentence.**
1. Sue is wearing a yellow dress. 2. She's wearing an orange belt, too. 3. Is she wearing purple boots? 4. What color is her cap?
• **Listen to Partner B say a sentence.** • **Listen again.** • **Complete the sentence.**
5. Felix is wearing a blue _____.
6. Kumi is wearing a _____ sweater.
7. They're wearing black _____, too.
8. Is it _____ today?

- FOLD HERE -

Partner B
• **Listen to Partner A say a sentence.** • **Listen again.** • **Complete the sentence.**
1. Sue is wearing a yellow _____.
2. She's wearing an _____ belt, too.
3. Is she wearing _____ boots?
4. What color is her _____?
• **Read a sentence to Partner A.** • **Repeat the sentence.** • **Watch Partner A complete the sentence.**
5. Felix is wearing a blue jacket. 6. Kumi is wearing a green sweater. 7. They're wearing black coats, too. 8. Is it snowing today?

Unit 10 Where's the Bank?

Places in the Community

1. Work with 3 classmates.

2. Label what you see in the picture.

3. Check your spelling in a dictionary.

post office

KEEP GOING!

Talk about the picture. Say what you see.

Where Is It?

1. Work with a partner.

2. Read the words in the box.

3. Look at the picture. Circle what you see.

apartment building	house	next to	across from
between	on the corner	~~restaurant~~	bank

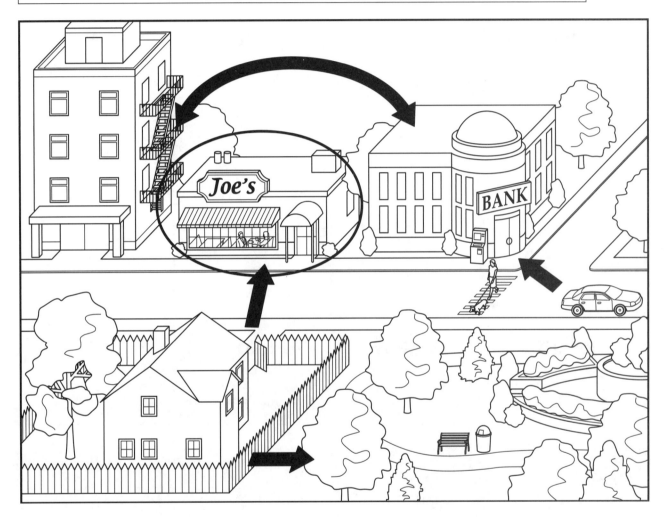

4. Look at the picture. Complete the sentences. Use *across from, next to,* or *between.*

There's a restaurant _____ the bank and the apartment building.

There's a restaurant _____ the house.

There's a park _____ the house.

KEEP GOING!

Work in a group. Write more about the picture.
There's a bank on the corner.

Sentence Maker

1. Work with a group of 3 or 4 students. Cut apart the cards.

2. Choose a Recorder.

3. Use the word cards to make 5 different sentences or questions in 10 minutes.
   The Recorder writes the group's sentences and questions.

THERE	IS	ARE	A
TWO	RESTAURANT	BOOKSTORE	SUPERMARKETS
BANKS	NEARBY	ACROSS	FROM
THE	NEXT	TO	ON
MAPLE	STREET	.	?

Where Is the Post Office?

1. Work with 2 classmates. Say all the lines in the script.
2. Choose your character.
3. Finish the conversation. Write more lines for the characters.
4. Practice the lines.
5. Act out the role-play with your group.

Scene	**Characters**	**Props**
A street corner	• Person 1 • Person 2 • Person 3	An envelope

The Script

Person 1: Excuse me. Where is the post office?

Person 2: It's between the bus station and the bookstore.

Person 3: Is it on Maple Street?

Person 2: Yes, it is. It's next to the supermarket.

Person 1: Is there a bank near the post office?

KEEP GOING!
Act out the role-play for your class.

In Your Community

1. Walk around the room.

2. Ask your classmates: *In your community, is there a* _____ *nearby?*

3. Write your classmates' names under their answers.

	Classmates' Names	
	Yes, there is.	**No, there's not.**
In your community, is there a Department of Motor Vehicles (DMV) nearby?		
In your community, is there a police station nearby?		
In your community, is there a fire station nearby?		
In your community, is there a hospital nearby?		
In your community, is there a courthouse nearby?		
In your community, is there a library nearby?		
In your community, is there a restaurant nearby?		
In your community, is there a park nearby?		

KEEP GOING!
Talk about this mixer with your class.

Picture Cards

1. Cut apart the picture cards. Use the word list to write the words on the back.

2. Work with a partner. Take turns.

   Partner A: Show the picture card to your partner.

   Partner B: Say the word.

3. Change roles.

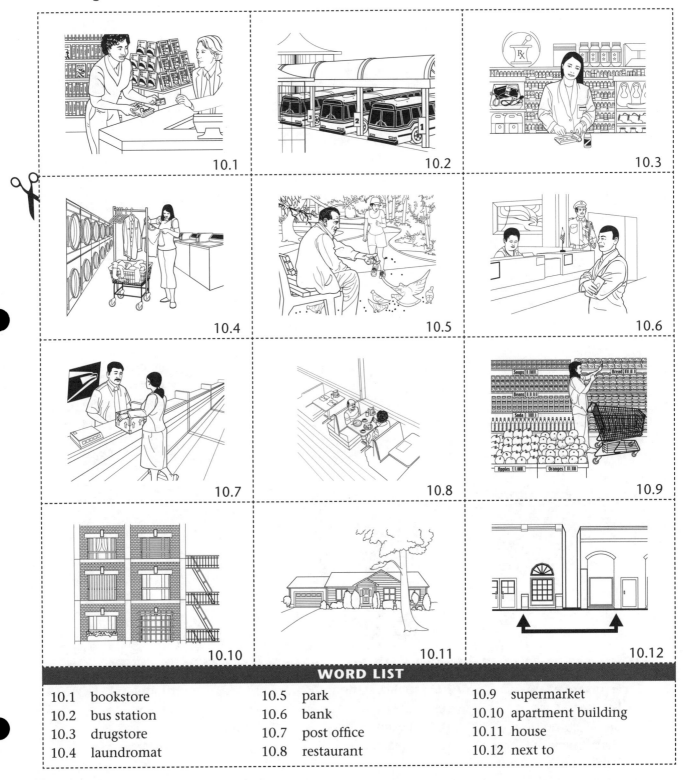

WORD LIST		
10.1 bookstore	10.5 park	10.9 supermarket
10.2 bus station	10.6 bank	10.10 apartment building
10.3 drugstore	10.7 post office	10.11 house
10.4 laundromat	10.8 restaurant	10.12 next to

Picture Cards

1. Cut apart the picture cards. Use the word list to write the words on the back.

2. Work with a partner.

    Partner A: Show the picture card to your partner.

    Partner B: Say the word.

3. Change roles.

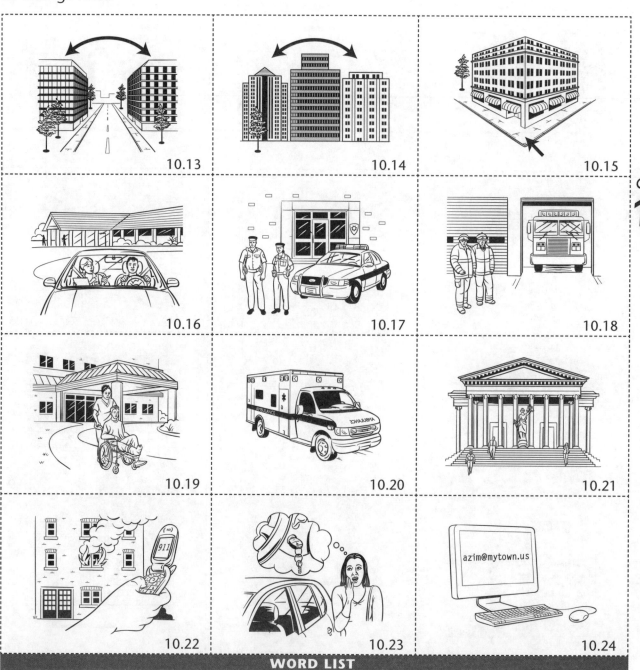

10.13	10.14	10.15
10.16	10.17	10.18
10.19	10.20	10.21
10.22	10.23	10.24

WORD LIST

10.13 across from	10.17 police station	10.21 courthouse
10.14 between	10.18 fire station	10.22 emergency
10.15 on the corner	10.19 hospital	10.23 non-emergency
10.16 Department of Motor Vehicles (DMV)	10.20 ambulance	10.24 email address

An Emergency on Pine Street

1. Work with your classmates.

2. Look at the picture.

3. Say what you see.

4. Watch your teacher write the story on the board or overhead.

5. Copy the story.

_____

_____

_____

_____

_____

_____

_____

What's Nearby?

Partner A
• **Read a sentence to Partner B.** • **Repeat the sentence.** • **Watch Partner B complete the sentence.**
1. Is there a restaurant nearby? 2. Yes, there is. 3. Is it on Elm Street? 4. Yes, it's across from the park.
• **Listen to Partner B say a sentence.** • **Listen again.** • **Complete the sentence.**
5. Is there a _____ nearby?
6. No, there's _____.
7. Is there a _____ nearby?
8. Yes, it's _____ to the bank.

- FOLD HERE -

Partner B
• **Listen to Partner A say a sentence.** • **Listen again.** • **Complete the sentence.**
1. Is there a _____ nearby?
2. Yes, there _____.
3. Is it _____ Elm Street?
4. Yes, it's across _____ the park.
• **Read a sentence to Partner A.** • **Repeat the sentence.** • **Watch Partner A complete the sentence.**
5. Is there a supermarket nearby? 6. No, there's not. 7. Is there a drugstore nearby? 8. Yes, it's next to the bank.

Unit 11 This Is My Home

I Like Your Furniture!

1. Work with 3 classmates.

2. Label what you see in the picture.

3. Check your spelling in a dictionary.

room

Above and Below

1. Work with a partner.

2. Read the words in the box.

3. Look at the picture. Circle what you see.

~~in~~	above	below	bedroom
bathroom	living room	kitchen	garage

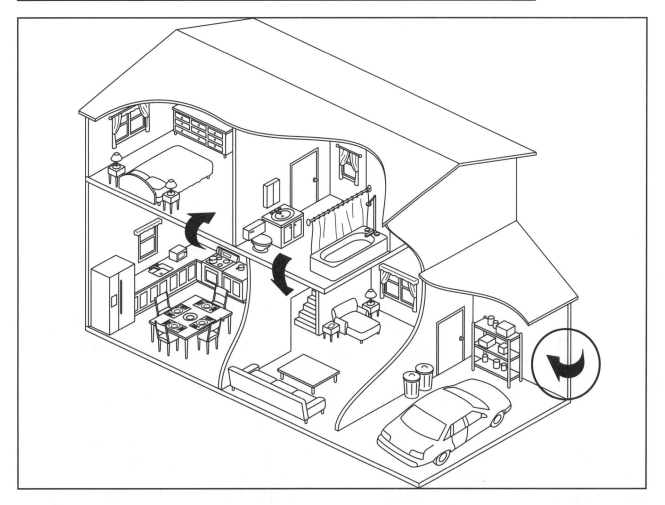

4. Look at the picture. Complete the sentences. Use *in, above,* or *below.*

The living room is _____ the bathroom.

The car is _____ the garage.

The bedroom is _____ the kitchen.

KEEP GOING!

Work in a group. Write more about the picture.
The bathroom is next to the bedroom.

Sentence Maker

1. Work with a group of 3 or 4 students. Cut apart the cards.

2. Choose a Recorder.

3. Use the word cards to make 5 different sentences or questions in 10 minutes.
The Recorder writes the group's sentences and questions.

PAT'S	HIS	HER	THEIR
LIVING ROOM	KITCHEN	BEDROOMS	BATHROOMS
SOFA	IS	SMALL	BIG
YELLOW	TWO	HOW	MANY
ARE	THERE	.	?

We're Looking for the Manager

1. Work with 2 classmates. Say all the lines in the script.

2. Choose your character.

3. Finish the conversation. Write more lines for the characters.

4. Practice the lines.

5. Act out the role-play with your group.

Scene

An apartment office

Characters

- Sam
- Manager
- Drew

Props

A newspaper

The Script

Sam: Excuse me. We're looking for the manager.

Manager: I'm the manager.

Drew: Nice to meet you. My name is Drew.

Sam: My name is Sam. Is there an apartment for rent?

Manager: Yes, there is. Rent is $800 a month.

Drew: That's cheap!

Sam: How many bedrooms are there?

Manager: Two.

Drew: How many bathrooms are there?

KEEP GOING!

Act out the role-play for your class.

What's in Your Living Room?

1. Walk around the room.

2. Ask your classmates: *Is there a _____ in your living room?*

3. Write *yes* or *no* in the boxes for your classmates.

	Classmate 1	Classmate 2	Classmate 3	Classmate 4	Classmate 5
Is there a sofa in your living room?					
Is there a TV in your living room?					
Is there a chair in your living room?					
Is there a table in your living room?					
Is there a desk in your living room?					
Is there a computer in your living room?					

KEEP GOING!

Talk about this mixer with your class.

Picture Cards

1. Cut apart the picture cards. Use the word list to write the words on the back.

2. Work with a partner.

Partner A: Show the picture card to your partner.

Partner B: Say the word.

3. Change roles.

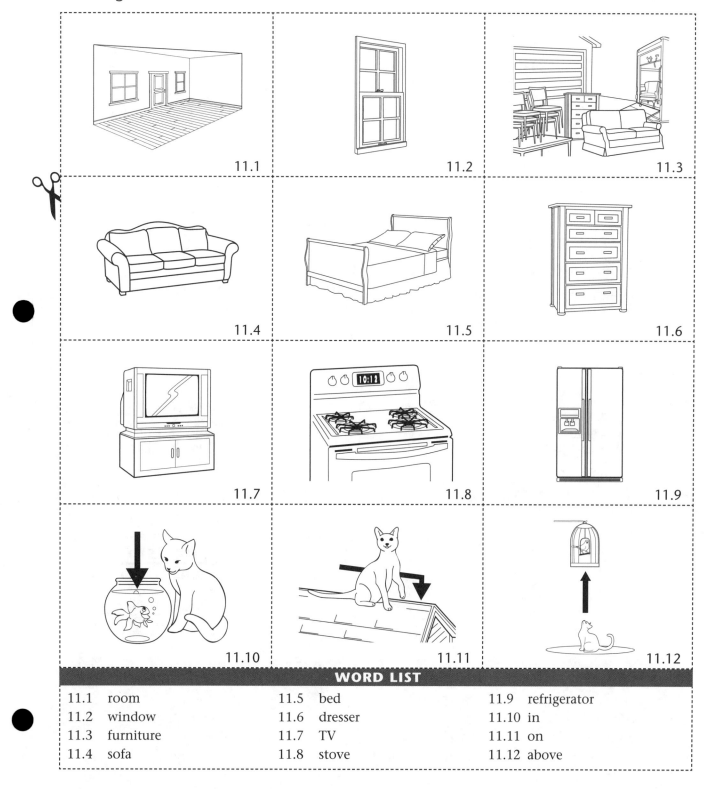

WORD LIST		
11.1 room	11.5 bed	11.9 refrigerator
11.2 window	11.6 dresser	11.10 in
11.3 furniture	11.7 TV	11.11 on
11.4 sofa	11.8 stove	11.12 above

Picture Cards

1. Cut apart the picture cards. Use the word list to write the words on the back.

2. Work with a partner.

Partner A: Show the picture card to your partner.

Partner B: Say the word.

3. Change roles.

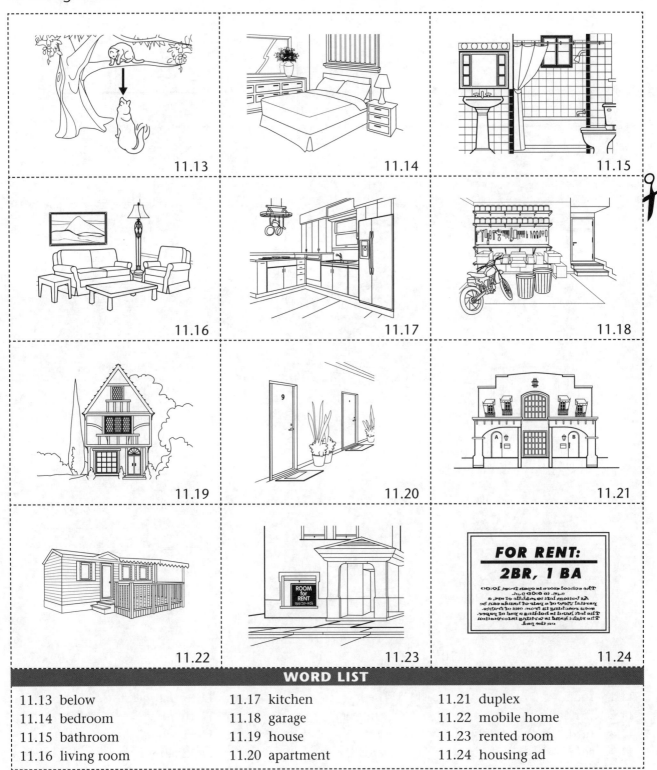

11.13

11.14

11.15

11.16

11.17

11.18

11.19

11.20

11.21

11.22

11.23

FOR RENT:
2BR, 1 BA

11.24

WORD LIST		
11.13 below	11.17 kitchen	11.21 duplex
11.14 bedroom	11.18 garage	11.22 mobile home
11.15 bathroom	11.19 house	11.23 rented room
11.16 living room	11.20 apartment	11.24 housing ad

An Apartment for Rent

1. Work with your classmates.

2. Look at the picture.

3. Say what you see.

4. Watch your teacher write the story on the board or overhead.

5. Copy the story.

_____

_____

_____

_____

_____

_____

_____

_____

This Is Their Home

Partner A
• **Read a sentence to Partner B.** • **Repeat the sentence.** • **Watch Partner B complete the sentence.**
1. My friends live in a house. 2. Their sofa is purple. 3. Their TV is in the bedroom. 4. They need a new refrigerator.
• **Listen to Partner B say a sentence.** • **Listen again.** • **Complete the sentence.**
5. George likes his _____.
6. His _____ room is big.
7. The _____ is small.
8. George's _____ is above a supermarket.

- FOLD HERE -

Partner B
• **Listen to Partner A say a sentence.** • **Listen again.** • **Complete the sentence.**
1. My friends live in a _____.
2. Their _____ is purple.
3. Their _____ is in the bedroom.
4. They need a new _____.
• **Read a sentence to Partner A.** • **Repeat the sentence.** • **Watch Partner A complete the sentence.**
5. George likes his apartment. 6. His living room is big. 7. The kitchen is small. 8. George's bedroom is above a supermarket.

Unit 12 Yes, I Can!

They Like Their Jobs

1. Work with 3 classmates.

2. Label what you see in the picture.

3. Check your spelling in a dictionary.

KEEP GOING!

Talk about the picture. Say what you see.

They Can Do It!

1. Work with a partner.

2. Read the words in the box.

3. Look at the picture. Circle what you see.

fix cars	drive trucks	cut hair	clean
take care of plants	paint houses	~~sell clothes~~	use computers

4. Look at the picture. Complete the sentences. Use *sell, use,* or *paint.*

Joe can _____ houses.

Alicia can _____ clothes.

She can _____ computers.

Sentence Maker

1. Work with a group of 3 or 4 students. Cut apart the cards.

2. Choose a Recorder.

3. Use the word cards to make 5 different sentences or questions in 10 minutes.
The Recorder writes the group's sentences and questions.

I	YOU	WE	THEY
HE	SHE	CAN	CAN'T
CLEAN	DRIVE	USE	FIX
SELL	PAINT	HOUSES	CARS
COMPUTERS	CLOTHES	.	?

I'm Here for a Job Interview

1. Work with 2 classmates. Say all the lines in the script.

2. Choose your character.

3. Finish the conversation. Write more lines for the characters.

4. Practice the lines.

5. Act out the role-play with your group.

Scene	Characters	Props 
An office	• Kim • Secretary • Manager	• A notebook • A pen

The Script

Kim: I'm here for a job interview.

Secretary: OK. What job is it for?

Kim: It's for the salesperson job.

Secretary: Can you tell me your name, please?

Kim: My name is Kim.

Secretary: One minute, please. Kim, this is the manager.

Manager: Good afternoon, Kim.

Kim: Nice to meet you.

Manager: Can you work on weekends?

Kim: Yes, I can.

Manager: Can you use computers?

KEEP GOING!

Act out the role-play for your class.

Work Questions

1. Walk around the room.

2. Ask your classmates: *Can you work* _____?

3. Write *yes* or *no* in the boxes for your classmates.

	Classmate 1	Classmate 2	Classmate 3	Classmate 4	Classmate 5
Can you work full-time?					
Can you work part-time?					
Can you work mornings?					
Can you work evenings?					
Can you work weekends?					

KEEP GOING!
Talk about this mixer with your class.

Picture Cards

1. Cut apart the picture cards. Use the word list to write the words on the back.
2. Work with a partner.
   Partner A: Show the picture card to your partner.
   Partner B: Say the word.
3. Change roles.

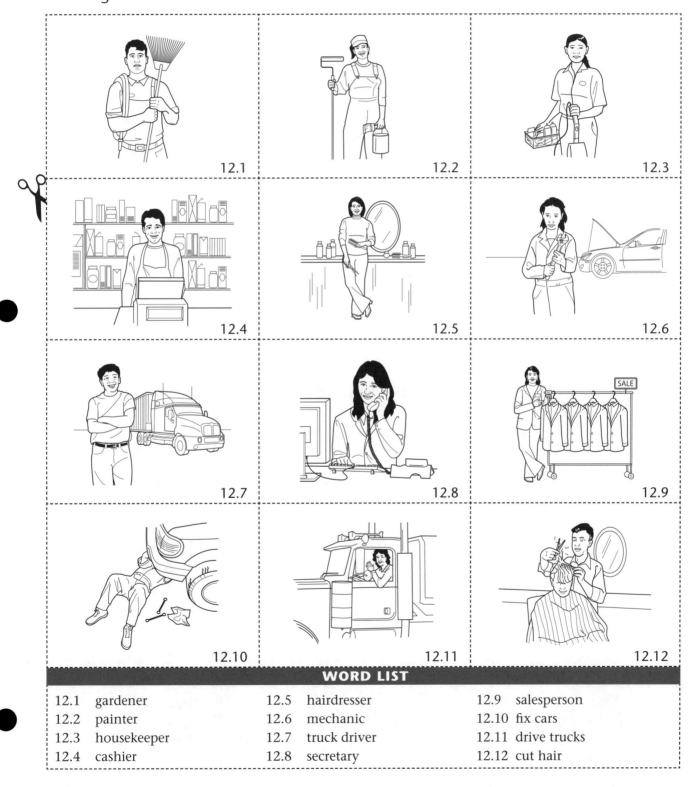

WORD LIST		
12.1 gardener	12.5 hairdresser	12.9 salesperson
12.2 painter	12.6 mechanic	12.10 fix cars
12.3 housekeeper	12.7 truck driver	12.11 drive trucks
12.4 cashier	12.8 secretary	12.12 cut hair

Picture Cards

1. Cut apart the picture cards. Use the word list to write the words on the back.

2. Work with a partner.

Partner A: Show the picture card to your partner.

Partner B: Say the word.

3. Change roles.

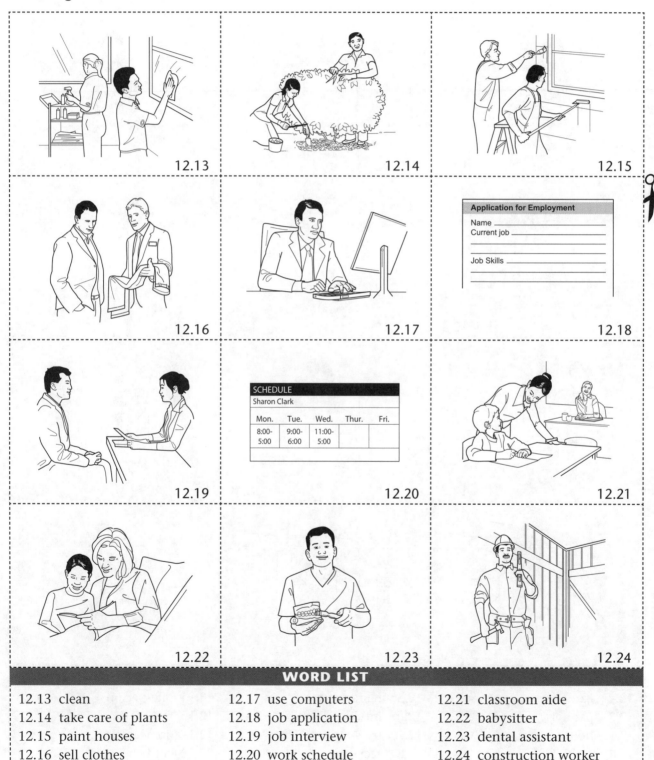

12.13

12.14

12.15

12.16

12.17

Application for Employment

Name

Current job

Job Skills

12.18

12.19

SCHEDULE
Sharon Clark

	Mon.	Tue.	Wed.	Thur.	Fri.
	8:00-5:00	9:00-6:00	11:00-5:00		

12.20

12.21

12.22

12.23

12.24

WORD LIST

12.13	clean	12.17	use computers	12.21	classroom aide
12.14	take care of plants	12.18	job application	12.22	babysitter
12.15	paint houses	12.19	job interview	12.23	dental assistant
12.16	sell clothes	12.20	work schedule	12.24	construction worker

Ed Is Looking for a Job

1. Work with your classmates.

2. Look at the picture.

3. Say what you see.

4. Watch your teacher write the story on the board or overhead.

5. Copy the story.

_____

_____

_____

_____

_____

_____

_____

_____

Job Skills

Partner A
• **Read a sentence to Partner B.** • **Repeat the sentence.** • **Watch Partner B complete the sentence.**
1. Tony's friends are mechanics. 2. They can fix his car. 3. He's a hairdresser. 4. He can cut their hair.
• **Listen to Partner B say a sentence.** • **Listen again.** • **Complete the sentence.**
5. I'm a _____.
6. I can _____ care of your plants.
7. You are a _____.
8. Can you _____ my house?

— FOLD HERE —

Partner B
• **Listen to Partner A say a sentence.** • **Listen again.** • **Complete the sentence.**
1. Tony's friends are _____.
2. They can _____ his car.
3. He's a _____.
4. He can _____ their hair.
• **Read a sentence to Partner A.** • **Repeat the sentence.** • **Watch Partner A complete the sentence.**
5. I'm a gardener. 6. I can take care of your plants. 7. You are a painter. 8. Can you paint my house?